A WOMAN'S GOLF GAME

Shirli Kaskie

Contemporary Books, Inc.
Chicago

Library of Congress Cataloging in Publication Data

Kaskie, Shirli.
  A woman's golf game.

  Includes index.
  1. Golf for women.   I. Title.
GV966.K37   1982   796.352′3′088042   81-69628
ISBN 0-8092-5757-2 (cloth)   AACR2
      0-8092-5756-4 (paper)

Published by Contemporary Books, Inc.
180 North Michigan Avenue, Chicago, Illinois 60601
Manufactured in the United States of America
Library of Congress Catalog Card Number: 81-69628
International Standard Book Number: 0-8092-5757-2 (cloth)
                                    0-8092-5756-4 (paper)

Published simultaneously in Canada by
Beaverbooks, Ltd.
150 Lesmill Road
Don Mills, Ontario M3B 2T5
Canada

Contents

The Ladies Professional Golf Association's first million-dollar winner.

Foreword

There's nothing like stepping onto a golf course on a clear fresh morning. The beauty and grace of the game of golf, its intellectual challenge, the fellowship with your playing partners—these qualities make it my favorite game. Although it is somewhat more than a game to me, being the way in which I make my living, I never cease to enjoy these basic qualities, which first drew me to golf.

Throughout my career, there have been other "basics" I have constantly returned to, the basics of the golf swing. Whenever I mishit a shot or notice a swing problem, I return to these basics of swing, stance, grip, and alignment. Too many of us complicate our golf swings with involved theories when good golf actually is based on a few simple principles.

In the following pages, some of the fellow players I most respect will relate these simple and basic theories to you. I think they will help you play better golf.

Kathy Whitworth

Introduction

Any woman can play golf. If you're 28 or 48, athletic or not, you can swing a golf club. This book brings together some of the top women golfers in the world to help you learn how.

The idea for this book developed because 18 years of amateur golf taught me that a woman's golf game is distinct from a man's. The way a woman approaches the game, the clubs she uses, and the way she hits the ball all differ from a man. Why shouldn't aspiring women golfers model their game after women pro golfers? Find out how the pros think about swinging a club, what the best way to spend time on a practice tee is, what the difference between hitting a ball on the fairway or in the rough is, and how to use the right clubs for certain shots. These are just some of the subjects the women pros in *A Woman's Golf Game* talk about.

If you're just taking up the game, these women have invaluable suggestions to make your learning easier and more satisfying. Low handicappers can benefit from the analytical advice on sharpening specific skills that the pros offer. There is helpful information here for every kind of golfer—even me. Using my new set of clubs and mumbling key words, I dropped my handicap three points while working on this book!

The Ladies Professional Golf Association

Golf is the business of the women in the Ladies Professional Golf Association (LPGA). They play competitively for money or teach at courses and golf shops across the country. From the original 11 members in 1951, the LPGA has grown to number 185 active women on the tour and 250 teaching members.

The women quoted in this book play on the LPGA tour. Since 1973 they have earned this privilege by meeting the requirements of the LPGA's qualifying schools, held twice a year. Each year more and more young women come to compete for a place on the tour.

The tour lasts from the end of January to the beginning of December. Almost every week a tournament is being held somewhere in the United States, as well as in Japan. At least 90 of the LPGA players participate in each scheduled event. The organization guarantees its tournament sponsors that a certain number of its top thirty players will appear in every competition.

1

Players arrive at the tournament site to register anytime between Monday morning and Wednesday morning. Mondays and Tuesdays are relaxed days. The pros munch on apples and sip soft drinks as they stroll to the practice tees. There they work with both woods and irons. They practice in bunkers. They putt. Some listen to instructors, who have come to help them analyze their game.

Wednesdays are usually Pro-Am days. The pros are teamed up to play with amateurs who have donated to a charity in order to play with a pro. Many amateurs say the women professional golfers are friendlier and just as much fun to play with as professional men golfers. The women seem to try harder to make the amateurs enjoy their game together.

Otherwise the pros don't socialize much with the people hosting the tournament. But they are not aloof. They have worked hard to get where they are. They are wise enough to appreciate the opportunity sponsors and golf club members give them to compete on some of the finest courses in the world.

Thursday is the starting day of the tournaments. After the first two days the field is cut down to the top 70 players with the lowest scores for the last two days' play.

There is a camaraderie between the players and the caddies. Some players have a regular caddy, who receives a weekly salary plus a percentage of the player's winnings. Others choose local caddies at each tournament.

These women are professional golfers. They love the game. It transcends everything they do. They are able to make a living doing it because they are members of the LPGA.

Meet the LPGA Players

AMY ALCOTT

Amy Alcott has won two major titles: in 1979 the Peter Jackson Classic and in 1980 the U.S. Women's Open. She was also awarded the 1980 Vare Trophy for her record of 101 games averaging 71.51. Amy believes that keeping in good shape is part of playing good golf. You could spot her jogging around a motel parking lot, not far from a tournament site, to get in her daily 2½–3 miles. This 25-year-old native Californian's desire to give something back to the game that has given so much to her led her to initiate her annual tournament in Los Angeles to benefit multiple sclerosis.

JERILYN BRITZ

Jerilyn Britz always wanted to become a professional athlete but took time to work up to it. She taught school and got her master's degree before arriving on the tour at age 30. This fair-haired pro appears laidback and easygoing, but her actions belie this image. A constant competitor, Jerilyn was the oldest player to make the U.S. Women's Open her first tournament victory. She's a friendly Midwesterner with a subtle sense of humor. She loves the "home away from home" feeling that traveling from tournament to tournament in her own van gives her.

BONNIE BRYANT

The LPGA's only left-handed golfer on the tour is right-handed otherwise. Bonnie took up the game when she was 20. If she hadn't played semipro softball as a left-hander, she wouldn't be a professional golfer today. The strong left side she had developed helped her earn a 5 handicap in just a couple of years. She's been on the tour for 11 years now, with her first tournament win in 1974. Four knee operations have limited Bonnie's continual participation on the tour, but she plans to leave her home in Kalamazoo, Michigan, to practice in Florida for the 1982 season.

BETH DANIEL

Being the first player to win more than $200,000 in a single season hasn't jaded 24-year-old Beth's excitement over a great shot. For an instant her reserve drops, her big brown eyes glisten, and she smiles with delight as the stellar drive she just sent far down the fairway goes exactly where she intended it. This tall southern lady from South Carolina was the 1979 Rookie of the Year and the 1980 Player of the Year. Off the course she's thoughtful, direct, and soft-spoken. On the course, at times she appears temperamental because she gets disgusted with herself and tends to be curt when her game isn't going well.

MARLENE FLOYD

Petite Marlene, with her golden blond naturally curly hair, seems almost too soft to be a professional golfer. Though the Floyds are a golfing family—her father's a teaching pro and brother, Ray, is a top PGA player—Marlene didn't take up the game seriously until she started dating a pro. To get some competitive experience she played amateur tournaments in between flights as an airline stewardess until she qualified for the tour in 1976. Marlene is a student of the game. She's read almost every book written on the subject. Her best year to date on the tour was 1981.

DOT GERMAIN

Under her soft, almost shy manner there lies the sterner stuff that brought Dot to her first tournament win and into the top 20 for the first time in 1980. Tall, with regal posture, reed-slim Dot glides placidly down the fairways, or so it appears. Born in Iowa, Dot was introduced to golf when she was only seven. Both her mother and her aunt were outstanding golfers. She owns her own home in Greensboro, North Carolina, and in the off-season goes back there to do a little housekeeping and see what's going on in the neighborhood.

SALLY LITTLE

Sally is the first player on the LPGA tour from South Africa. She was a top international player but says she learned the sterner qualities of competitive play after she joined the LPGA tour in 1971. Her victories since then include the 1980 LPGA. The caddies refer to Sally as a "first class lady." She is quite reserved until she starts talking about the game of golf. Then her enthusiasm breaks through in clipped British phrases. Sally is naturally left-handed, but her father taught her to play golf right-handed. Home is in Florida now, where she's expanding her interest in interior design.

NANCY LOPEZ

Nancy receives the acclaim of a star whenever she appears on the course. But she has no such affectations. She is warm, unsophisticated, and unassuming—yet fully in command of herself and her situation. She is humble about her achievements. After two years of college she joined the tour in 1977 and proceeded to set new records for rookie earnings, official monies, and scoring averages. She won the 1978 LPGA, but her string of five wins in a row in 1979 has been her most noteworthy accomplishment. Nancy lives in Houston, Texas.

SANDRA PALMER

Sandra is so small that it's hard to imagine she was a teen-age caddy in Maine. Now a Texan, she's acquired a Southern drawl. Sandra approaches her game with a "strictly business" attitude. She is the player you see early in the week of a tournament, stalking the course alone or with her caddy, meticulously measuring her yardages, practicing her shots. She's a friendly tease after she gets to know you. Since joining the tour in 1964, Sandra has been in the top 10 most of the time. Her list of victories includes the 1975 U.S. Women's Open.

JUDY RANKIN

This blue-eyed, platinum blond from Texas is one of the most familiar players on the tour. In 1982 Judy will celebrate 20 years as a professional golfer. She grew up in St. Louis and joined the tour when she was 17. In 1976 she became the first $100,000 winner. "My back injury in 1973, then again in 1977—no one knows what that did to my game," she says. But she's not retiring. Playing in only 17 tournaments in 1980, Judy amassed more than $50,000. On the tour she works on her game and crossword puzzles. She calls home daily to check on how her husband and 13-year-old son Tuey are doing.

ALISON SHEARD

Alison is an international player on the tour from Durban, South Africa, shuttling between the states and Europe to play in golf tournaments. She won the 1979 British Women's Open. One of her high moments was finding an antique putter that once belonged to Tommy Armour. One of her lowest was having to have it cut down to be able to use it. Between seasons she goes back home to South Africa to do some teaching.

HOLLIS STACY

Hollis is as open and friendly as her smile. An easygoing Georgia girl, she made history on the tour when she became only the fourth player ever to win consecutive U.S. Women's Open tournaments in 1977 and 1978. She's been winning consistently and has been high on the money list since 1977, three years after she joined the tour. Her mother was her first teacher. Now she coaches her two sisters to follow in her footsteps. Off-season, Hollis loves to fish and travel. So far an African safari has been her high point of adventure. Her home now is in Hilton Head, South Carolina.

MYRA VAN HOOSE

Myra has a wide selection of caps she frequently wears around the course during a tournament that pretty well hide her vivid brown eyes and hair. She started her career off being named the 1980 Rookie of the Year. After the season she married. With her husband as her caddy and advisor, she is back on the tour trying to match the success of her initial year. She is enthused and articulate about golf. She just finds it a little difficult to explain how a Kentucky girl with a degree in agriculture ended up being a professional golfer on the LPGA tour.

KATHY WHITWORTH

Kathy staged a valiant charge to win her first U.S. Women's Open in 1981. If the rains hadn't come on the final Sunday, she might have done it. She needed hard, dry fairways to keep the lead she had held since the opening round. However, her third place finish did make her the first million-dollar winner on the LPGA tour. A victory would have tied her with Mickey Wright for the most tour titles ever. But she's not quitting yet. During her 22 years of competition she's won 80 times, including three LPGA titles. Already ensconced in the LPGA's Hall of Fame, Kathy is regarded with as much affection as respect by her tour competitors.

MARIE FEENEY—THE RULES EXPERT

Marie has become an expert in her hobby, the rules of golf. She took the PGA–USGA Rules in Depth Workshop in 1977 and scored a 96 on the final exam. When she participated in the LPGA's Rules Seminar in 1981, she scored another 96. As Rules Chairman for the Chicago Women's District Golf Association for a number of years, Marie has had ample opportunities for practical application of her expertise. She also plays a sharp amateur game, carding a 16 handicap at Evanston Golf Club in Illinois. Now that the Feeneys have moved to Vero Beach, Florida, Marie will be playing at John's Island Club.

A Salute to Patty Berg

Patty Berg's red hair is white now and her freckles have turned golden with 63 years. But she was in the grandstand on the 18th green at the 36th U.S. Women's Open in LaGrange, Illinois, in July 1981.

As young, new players walked off the green, she made a point to go over and talk to them about their game, about how they were doing. Former playing partners ran over to hug her when they saw her. More recent comers on the tour came over to shake hands with this lady who did so much to bring the game they love to the forefront of women's professional athletics.

Patty Berg has fun boasting that she's been selling sporting goods for 42 years. But that's not what made her the women's golf legend that she is.

Together with Betty Jameson, Louise Suggs, and Babe Zaharias, Patty founded the LPGA in 1950. She was its first elected president. After winning the U.S. Amateur title in

1938, Patty went on to win more than 80 titles after she turned pro in 1940. In August 1978 the LPGA established the Patty Berg Award for outstanding contributions to women's golf.

Looking back, Patty observes, "Junior golf has made the big change in women's golf. Now, before a girl turns professional, she's had from four to six years of competitive golf, if she wants it.

"Athletes are stronger now. Thanks to their interest in food—vitamins and minerals—women know more about what is good for their body and what isn't. That, too, is progress."

Age, a cancer operation, and hip surgery haven't diminished Patty's enthusiasm for this game she's taught and played for almost half a century.

"Golf has no age limit. You can play it as long as you wish," she declares. And she still does. Almost daily, late in the afternoon, when she's at home in Fort Myers, Florida, Patty slips out to play a round or a few holes, depending on how she feels.

As she sat in the sunshine, Patty commented, "That's really the great thing about golf, you know. You meet so many great people."

Patty Berg is the personification of *A Woman's Golf Game.*

Time has faded Patty Berg's red hair, but none of her enthusiasm for women's golf. She came to the 36th U.S. Women's Open in July 1981 to cheer on former competitors and encourage the new ones.

1
Taking Up the Game

There is nothing natural about swinging a golf club. That's why you don't have to be athletic to learn how. It is also why trying to learn on your own won't work unless you are an exceptional athlete.

IMITATE

You can learn to swing a golf club by imitating good players.

"The easiest way to learn to play is through imitation," Beth Daniel believes. "Swinging a club is such an unnatural move that imitating someone who hits the ball well can be an easy way to learn. You can watch someone and say to yourself, 'I don't follow through like she does.' And so you try to do what she does."

"For our size and weight, we women pros do hit the ball far," Sally Little observes. "From watching us play you learn that you have to have a lot of coordination to hit the ball so far."

20

Attitude and composure are other factors in a pro's game worth imitating, Sandra Palmer comments. "Anger has no place on the course. All it does is hurt you."

Watching the LPGA tournaments on TV or attending one when you have a chance offers you a great opportunity to watch the best women golfers in the world swing their clubs. And don't overlook attending amateur tournaments in your area—a convenient way to watch good women amateur golfers play.

Study the pictures of the women pros on the pages of this book. Observe their position at address, when they are setting up to hit the ball; note their arms on their backswing; see how their swing follows through. You can study such details of swing and set in your mind a visual image of a good one.

READ

Since you have this book in hand, you are aware that you can learn a great deal about the golf swing and the game by reading about them. If you are a beginner, studying the ingredients of a good golf swing as you are learning it reemphasizes the various skills you are trying to acquire.

Veteran players frequently pick up golf books to remind themselves of the basics of a good golf swing when they are having problems or their swing doesn't feel right. Even pros occasionally get back to the basics when something goes wrong in their swing.

INSTRUCTION

Once you've made up your mind that you're going to learn to play golf, go to a professional golf instructor. Even if your boyfriend has a 2 handicap and has been helping you, or your husband has been teaching you his secrets, you will learn easier and more accurately from an instructor because he or she is a professional teacher.

A good instructor can offer you two or three ways to think about a golf swing, if necessary, to be certain you understand what you have to do to hit a golf ball solidly with a golf club.

Amy Alcott found her instructor at an indoor driving range near her home in southern California. You can find yours through your park district, at a public golf course, through an outdoor driving range, or through night school classes. Some pros at private clubs also teach nonmembers, if asked.

"If you can afford only one lesson," Nancy Lopez advises, "tell the pro you want it on the fundamentals: the grip, the stance, and alignment."

Amy Alcott suggests, "Try to take at least one lesson to learn how to grip the club and take it back. Taking even one lesson helps. You'll enjoy learning more with some direction."

You might be able to do as Beth Daniel proposes: "Join a weekly golf clinic, which is cheaper than individual lessons. At each clinic the pro teaches a different part of the game— one week chipping, the next week putting, then the short irons, the woods, and so on."

If you have the time and money, you might try a week's vacation at a golf resort to learn whether golf is your sport or not. These resorts offer group lessons for their guests. Learning with other people allows you to benefit from their mistakes and instruction as well as your own. An added plus: the instructor rates you on your progress on a day-to-day basis. It's an intensive sort of instruction that can get you off to a good start on your game.

A WOMAN'S GAME

Some women assume golf is a game of power. Men do hit the ball farther and are able to hit the ball right or hit it left to work it around better than women, because they are stronger. But a woman can play the game as well as a man. She just plays it differently. Golf is not a game of power for a woman. It is a game of accuracy. Accuracy is, in fact, the most important factor in a woman's game.

If you were to compare a woman and a man with equal handicaps hitting a five iron to the green, you'd probably see the man hitting his shot from about 170 yards out and the woman hitting hers from 110 to 120 yards out, more or less. This difference, however, is not important.

The point of the game is to get the ball into the hole in the fewest number of strokes possible. Your sex does make a difference in what club you choose to make a shot, but not in the number of strokes you take to get your ball into the hole. And that's what you put on your score card.

APPROACHING THE GAME

So when are you ready to walk onto a course to play golf? Probably when you can consistently hit a ball up in the air with your five or seven iron.

Start swinging the shorter irons on the practice range to get the feel of swinging the clubs and contacting the ball. But until you can swing a seven iron over and over on the practice range and always hit the ball squarely and solidly, you shouldn't consider going to a regular course to play. You will become extremely frustrated with yourself and the players with you and behind you will, too.

Why not approach taking up the game as some of the women pros have done? Sally Little's dad had her learn to chip with the short irons first. She developed a feel for the clubs that way and didn't become discouraged trying to hit shots she couldn't handle. She didn't go out on a course until she knew how to hit each club.

"You can spend the winter on an inside practice range just learning how to hit the different clubs," she notes. "You don't have to be outdoors to learn and you don't have to be in a hurry. Take your time. Get better at hitting each club one by one."

Or you might consider starting out with your putter, as Jerilyn Britz suggests. "The putting stroke is the golf swing in miniature. If you can get a good stroke down, develop confidence in it; that's a big help. You can always make up for a lot of mistakes out on the fairway if you can putt well."

ON THE PRACTICE RANGE

It's unanimous. All the women pros advise: begin working on your golf swing on the practice range, probably with a seven iron. The longer clubs are harder to learn how to swing. Start with the clubs that are easier to hit with and work down to the most difficult—from the nine iron to the seven iron, to the five iron, to the seven wood, to the five wood, to the three wood. Only when you're playing fairly well should you start using your driver.

How much you improve, how quickly you play fairly well, depends on how much time you can spend practicing. Golf is a difficult game to play well. It takes time and patience to learn.

Initially on the practice range both Marlene Floyd and Sandra Palmer propose that you hit with a tee under the ball. When the ball sits down on the ground you often try to help it up into the air. There is a tendency to try to scoop the ball up into the air instead of freely swinging the club and letting its clubface put the ball into the air. Teeing the ball up will give you the necessary confidence to hit the ball and get it airborne. You can acquire tempo with the ball teed up. Then, when you get all the balls popping up and out nicely, put the ball down on the ground.

Sandra Palmer explains what happens. "In order for the ball to get up into the air, you have to get the bottom of the arc of your swing at the ball. Get the bottom of the arc where the ball is—that's the ideal for every shot. So, when you put the ball on the tee it's easier to hit the ball at that spot. You aren't afraid of hitting the ground. You're not trying to pick the ball up with your club. You're learning to swing the club freely, naturally contacting the ball at the bottom of the arc. Learn to hit all the clubs this way. When you are able to hit the balls off the ground with all your clubs on the practice range you will be able to do the same thing on the golf course."

If you look at the practice range as Marlene Floyd does, you see it as a chance for exercise and relaxation as well as a place to hit golf balls. Bending down and teeing up all those balls can help you lose weight and inches from your waist and hips. If your friend, husband, or child wants to come along with you to hit the balls, it can be fun, too.

ON THE COURSE

Even if you haven't mastered all the clubs when you go out on the course to play, you will enjoy the game if you can accept the level at which you play. You will improve as you are able to practice and think about your shots.

Nevertheless, you can always look around you on any course and enjoy the trees, the sky, the birds, the friends you're playing with. If you can play only once a week or less, so be it. Your progress will be slow. Be happy with the one good shot out of ten that you hit, rather than frustrated by the nine you missed. Don't think that you are worse than you are. Being overcompetitive takes the fun out of the game for too many amateurs.

"While you are learning, if you get a bad lie you don't like, move the ball," suggests Jerilyn Britz. "If your ball lands behind a tree and you don't know how to get out, throw the ball out. Of course, if you are where you have an opportunity to learn how to hit out of the bad lie or from behind the tree, practice the shots there."

You don't have to keep score every time you play when you are beginning the game. That's very frustrating. You find yourself more concerned with what you lie rather than how to hit your next shot. You can see how you're improving if you keep score occasionally, depending on how often you can play.

When Jerilyn's mother gets tired of counting strokes, when mother and daughter are playing a few holes together, she picks up her ball, then drops it on the green to putt.

The only time you have to hit every shot in golf is when you are playing in a competitive event or playing to establish or keep an official USGA handicap.

Enjoy learning to play golf. Don't let concern about getting better make your day on the course a frustrating experience. Your game will improve steadily and markedly from season to season as you play more and become familiar with your clubs.

Golf is not an easy game. You can only expect from it what you put into it. But do enjoy the game as you work to improve your shots.

EQUIPMENT

The kind of equipment you use does have an effect on your swing, but not until you consistently hit the ball well.

When you're taking up the game, use whatever type of clubs you can afford. Initially, you might use someone's old clubs or buy a secondhand set to see how you like the game. How rapidly you improve will dictate what you need in clubs.

When you are ready to invest in clubs that you want to use for a few years, it is most important to find the clubs that are right for you. Chapter 14, "Equipment," offers you detailed, practical, up-to-date information on what to look for in clubs and what is available for women. For too long, amateur women golfers had to play with clubs that were originally designed for men. This has changed. You can now buy clubs specially designed for women that really will help you play better golf. And to play well you must use proper equipment.

USING YOUR HEAD

Using your head means being aware of the mental game of golf. Concentration *does* affect your shots. If your mind is on the problems you left at the office or what the kids are doing at home, it will be hard to score well. You have to think about your shots before you hit them in order to hit them well.

You also have to learn to think about where you are going to try to place your ball when you hit it. What side of the fairway leaves you an open shot to the green? Which way will the ball roll when it hits the green? Those are just a couple of aspects of the mental game of golf.

WARM-UP

Then there is your body. Sometimes, after you've played a few holes, your poor body aches terribly. It's not unnatural for inactive muscles to ache after sudden, vigorous use. If you've been sitting at a desk all week or haven't played for a week or so, it's a good idea to do some bending and stretching exercises before you walk onto the first tee. It's a good idea to do them every time you are going to play, in fact.

The pros warm up, your club champ does it, and most of the better golfers do. Loosen up before you play. Athletes in all sports warm up before they play to help loosen muscles, sharpen coordination, and relax the mind, releasing it from other thoughts.

Here are some warm-up benders and stretchers that you can do before you play.

1. Take a couple of short irons and just swing them together, back and forth a few times, using a baseball grip. Don't swing fast. You just want the weight of the clubs to help loosen your back, shoulders, legs, and arms.

2. Swing one club freely, from the wrist with your left arm, then with both arms, to simulate the feel of the swing and to loosen up your arms.

Swing one club back and forth with your left arm only, then with both arms, a few times before you tee up on the first hole. Swing easily, freely, to get a feeling of the swing going.

3. Take a club and hold it behind you at the base of your back with your elbows over it. Bend back and forth a few times; twist and turn. Then hold the club out behind your back with your arms extended and bend up and down, sideways and back, a few times.

Put your club behind you with your elbows over it. Wrap your arms around the ends of it. Then bend and twist a few times before you play to loosen up those muscles between your shoulder blades.

Hold your club out behind you with your arms extended and your hands gripping both ends of it. Twist and turn, bend up and down, to loosen your arm muscles.

All this only takes a few minutes. But it could prevent muscle strain you might otherwise suffer.

Other activities can serve as effective warm-ups, as long as you don't overdo them. If you hit balls on the practice range to warm up, for example, don't swing hard. If your time is limited, take out your favorite iron and hit a few balls. Then pick your favorite wood and do the same.

If you can spend more time, you can start with your highest iron and hit a couple of shots with it, working down to your three or four iron. Then pull out your highest wood and work down to your driver, swinging a few times with each. Just get the feel of the clubs. Warm-up time isn't the time to work on your swing.

A little practice putting beforehand won't do much to loosen your muscles, but it can help your putting. It reminds you of the feel of your stroke.

No woman, except the pros, should play golf for any reason other than love of the game, a desire to have fun and relax. When you walk onto a course knowing how to swing a club, loosened up and confident, you are ready to do just that.

Enough of the preliminaries to playing golf. Now let's get down to the fundamentals.

How do you develop a swing? How do you hit the various woods and irons to play the game of golf? Read on.

2
The Basic Swing

No matter what club you use, the basics of a good golf swing are the same. Understanding just what these basics are and why they are so important to a good swing helps you make them a part of your swing.

THE GRIP

The grip—how you hold a golf club—is a vital part of every good swing. As a matter of fact, you *must* grip a golf club correctly, to be able to swing it well.

To grip your golf club properly, place the sole of the club flush with the ground, with the top of the shaft pointing upward toward you. A couple of inches from the top, lay the club across the palm of your left hand.

The Basic Overlap Grip

To grasp the club, Myra Van Hoose says, "Put your fingers

around the grip of the club with your left thumb straight
down the shaft just to the right of the center. Hold the club
primarily with the last three fingers of your left hand." The V
between your thumb and forefinger will be pointing toward
your right shoulder.

*With Myra Van Hoose's basic overlap grip, you see that the V
between her left thumb and index finger points toward her right
shoulder. Her left thumb is straight down, left of center, and the last
three fingers firmly hold the club. Her right hand is placed lightly
over her left thumb. Its pinkie nestles between the left middle and
index fingers. Her right thumb comes around to the left side of
center to rest lightly on her right index finger.*

Then place your right hand squarely against the shaft, just below your left hand. Bend your fingers around the club with your pinkie resting between your left forefinger and middle finger. Place your thumb left of center on the shaft. The pressure of your right hand on the club is applied by the thumb and forefinger. But it is a light pressure, as you would use to hold a butterfly. The right thumb and forefinger give you the feel of the club in your hands.

Keep in mind that the right hand steadies the left. And the pinkie is the main contact between your two hands; it keeps them working together.

Dot Germain holds her club up to show the underside of the overlap grip. Notice how the last three fingers of her left hand grip the club, where her right pinkie is, and how her right thumb rests against her right index finger.

A Stronger Grip

Both Sandra Palmer and Judy Rankin favor a stronger grip for women because it helps you hold your club more firmly at the top of the backswing. If you want to grip your club more strongly, turn your left hand slightly more toward your right when you grasp the club initially.

A note of caution about using this grip, however: Sometimes it can creep into your iron game and cause you to hook your shots into the green.

Experiment on the practice range with the regular grip and this stronger one. That is the only reliable way to find out which works best for you. Remember, golf is a highly individual game.

Here's the stronger overlap grip Judy Rankin favors. Both her left and right hands are turned more to the right on her club than Myra's. The knuckles of Judy's left hand are more visible, her right thumb more centered on her club.

Myra's basic stance for fairway woods is about shoulder width, square with the ball. Her upper body bends slightly forward at the waist, as her head naturally bends and her knees flex. She positions her ball somewhat farther back in her stance than some players might for these fairway shots.

STANCE

Stance refers to where you place your feet in relation to the clubhead and the ball.

To be able to swing freely, stand with your feet about shoulder width apart. Flex your legs slightly at the knees. Bend your upper body forward slightly from your waist. Your head will naturally bend a little, too, but be sure to limit this to a slight incline.

For most shots your feet should be "square," that is, they should be parallel from side to side and from toe to heel, like the four sides of a rectangle.

The term *open stance* means that you draw your left foot back a little from your right foot. The term *closed stance* means that you draw your right foot back from your left foot.

BALL POSITION

Most clubs in your bag call for the ball to be positioned off your left heel. "When you start moving the ball very much off your left heel for different shots you complicate your game," warns Sally Little. Hollis Stacy finds it easier to think of this position as the spot in line with her left ear.

Just how far back from the ball you should take your stance depends on how long your upper body is and how long your arms are.

To find that distance for yourself, Beth Daniel suggests that you stand with your arms extended in front of you from the shoulders, gripping your club as you ordinarily would. Bending at the waist, bring the club down. The spot where the bottom of the club comes to rest is about where your ball should be positioned in terms of distance from your body.

Basically, whatever feels comfortable to you is correct.

As Marlene Floyd checks her alignment, her ball is positioned off her left heel. That is the favored ball position for most shots.

Lay two clubs down in front of you—one in front of your feet and one on the line formed between your ball and the target—to check your alignment. Those clubs should be parallel, like a railroad track, if your alignment is correct.

ALIGNMENT

Alignment refers to the way your feet, your ball, and your clubhead are lined up with the target. It is the factor in a good swing that determines whether or not you hit the ball where you want it to go.

Marlene Floyd compares alignment in the golf swing to a railroad track. The ball in front of you and the flagstick straight ahead on the green form the line of flight for your ball to follow. Think of this line as the top railroad track. Your shoulders, body, and feet, standing parallel to that line of flight, form the bottom railroad track.

To align yourself correctly, place your clubface square with the ball on the line of flight to the target. Square your feet and make sure they are parallel to the line of flight. It is not possible to aim both the ball and your body directly at the target. If your body is aimed at the target, your ball will land to the right of it. So, line up your ball and clubhead with the target. Your body and feet, on the other hand, will be parallel to the line of flight.

HAND AND ARMS

To address the ball, put your clubhead up to the ball. Your hands should be slightly ahead of the ball (closer to the target). Beth Daniel positions her hands at the crease in the left leg of her slacks. Be certain that your left arm is straight, forming a continuous straight line extending from your shoulder to the shaft of the club to the clubface at the ball.

Bend your right arm in toward your body.

Keep your grip firm, but relax your arms. It's impossible to swing freely if your arms are tense.

At address, Sally Little's left arm extends in a straight line from her shoulder down to the clubface. Her right elbow is bent slightly in toward her body. Her hands are just a little ahead of the clubface. Her ball is farther back in her stance to play a shot out of the rough.

As Marlene starts to bring her club back, her weight begins to shift off her left foot to her right.

FOOTWORK

Footwork in a golf swing refers to how you shift your weight. First you transfer it from your left foot to your right, when you take your club back and up from the ball for your backswing. Then you shift your weight back to your left foot as you swing forward.

"Any woman who can dance can easily learn the footwork of a golf swing," Marlene Floyd declares. Describing the elements of footwork, Marlene continues, "You shift your weight from the left heel to the right heel as you take the club back, then from the right heel to the left as you bring the club forward."

our weight should shift from
ot to the outside of the right
t knee bends inward slightly
our backswing your weight
oot. As your hands set at the
starts to shift back to the
rn your body and shoulder
d your weight comes firmly
el. When you complete your
your right foot is on the

the top of Marlene's backswing, the weight is off her
left foot. Her left heel is off the ground, her knee bent slightly
inward. You see that her weight is firmly on her right foot. Below,
right: As Marlene starts her downswing, her weight shift back to the
left initiates. Her left heel is back on the ground. There is a forward
thrust to her left leg.

Above, left: As Marlene extends through the ball, her right foot lifts. Her left foot rolls over to carry the weight of her forward motion. Above, right: As Marlene completes her follow-through, only the toe of her right foot remains on the ground. All of her weight is to her left, leading her clubhead through to the target.

That's what the footwork of the golf swing is all about. If you can learn it properly, you will be in a perfect swing plane 90 percent of the time, Marlene finds. Your arms will swing up and down, following the rotation of your body and hips.

Judy Rankin reaffirms Marlene's conviction about the importance of footwork in a woman's swing. "The first and most important thing a woman must do in order to make a good swing is to learn good weight shift. That is, to shift your weight to your right side and then back to your left side when you swing a golf club. To hit a ball any distance, a woman cannot just stand there and hit the ball with her arms and hands the way some men do. A woman just isn't strong enough to do that."

Some instructors do try to teach women and children to swing primarily with their arms and shoulders without using their lower body. But the LPGA players believe a woman should try to learn to use her lower body in order to hit a ball well and far for a number of years.

Watch any of the pros on the LPGA tour in person or on TV. Study their pictures in this book. You'll see how each player uses her lower body in her swing. She shifts her weight from side to side to hit the ball as far as she does.

RHYTHM AND TEMPO

Rhythm and tempo—the timing of a golf swing—easily hold your attention when you watch the women professional golfers play. When you watch the male pros, you admire their power. But watching the women, you admire their rhythm and tempo, their grace which seems to create effortless power.

"To find rhythm in your swing, take your seven iron in your left hand and just swing it back and forth a few times," Hollis Stacy suggests. "You can't swing the club too fast with just one hand, and you can feel tempo. Then, when you put your right hand on it, keep that same feeling.

"As you hit balls from the practice tee, try to get the feel of rhythm in your swing. My mother told me to hum 'The Blue Danube' as I swung, to get the feel of rhythm in my swing. That helped me a lot. Why not hum 'The Blue Danube' while you're swinging your golf clubs? Working on nice rhythm that way will keep you from trying to kill the ball."

Counting out loud is the way Marlene Floyd works on rhythm. You count "one, two" on the backswing; pause at the top of the backswing; then count "three" for the downswing. That pause in the count allows your club the time to change direction at the top of the backswing, to get your weight shift going. With the count of "three" you can swing the club just as hard and fast as you want. But Marlene emphasizes, "You must give the club time to change direction at the top of the backswing." Other players refer to the point at the top of the backswing as the moment to cock your wrists or get set for the downswing.

Alison Sheard goes back to Tommy Armour's routine to teach rhythm when she is working with students in South Africa. Count "one, two" on the backswing; say "and" to allow the hands to cock at the top of the swing; "three" to come down.

Alison advises her young golfers to start cocking their hands at hip level and go on up until the club is about parallel to the ground. For older beginners she recommends cutting the swing down to bring the top of the backswing to the shoulder level.

The important thing is to develop rhythm in your current swing—not to be concerned about the extent of your backswing.

"If you don't have rhythm in your swing, you're not going to be consistent," says Sally Little. "Each woman has to develop her own tempo. Some women naturally move more quickly than others. You develop the rhythm for your swing from your own built-in tempo. You have to find out what is too fast a swing or too slow a swing. And then, what is just right for you."

ACCELERATION

Acceleration describes the clubhead speed as the club comes through the ball.

"Watching the women pros play, it is apparent that you have to have a lot of coordination to hit the ball far. For our size and weight we do hit the ball far," comments Sally Little. "When I swing with coordination and timing I am hitting the ball hard. I am conscious of acceleration. I have to be to hit the ball hard."

How does a woman get acceleration in her swing? Sally offers an explanation. "You have to time your swing correctly to hit the ball hard. If you don't complete the backswing, coming back down you don't have the speed you could have.

To complete her backswing Sally Little turns, with her left arm extended, until her shoulder is under her chin. Then she sets her wrists.

"I am at the top of my backswing when I take a complete full turn and set my hands at the top. It happens automatically as I turn as far as I can with my left arm extended until my left shoulder is under my chin. My wrist automatically cocks at the top then. It sets."

Judy Rankin agrees that acceleration comes with proper synchronization of movement, not from trying to make the clubhead move fast on its way to the ball. She offers an example to illustrate her point. "I can slap you and make it hurt much more than if I sock you. When I slap you, I cock my wrist and let my hand go as fast as it can. To sock you, I pull back and try to create force to hit you. But I really don't have much strength, so that sock doesn't hurt nearly as much as if I slap you."

That is why a man's swing differs from a woman's. A man packs a wallop if he socks you because his body has inherent strength. Judy can never hit a ball as far as Tom Watson. She relies on rhythmic coordination of movement to hit the ball well. Tom combines his strength with the same coordination

Above, left: This photo shows the long flat area in Judy Rankin's swing where her ball sits waiting for impact. Her acceleration coming through is evident in the weight shift of her lower body to her left. Her upper body, her shoulders, her arms are behind the ball to bring the club through. Above, right: As her club solidly strikes the ball, Judy's momentum continues. Her arms extend through, following her shoulders.

to hit a ball well. If his coordination is off, he can still hit a powerful shot because of his strength. Judy can't.

The same holds true for acceleration in a woman's golf swing. It happens when you really let the club go and swing. You can't force it just as you come to the ball, because you don't have the necessary strength.

"Swing the club. Swing the club freely through the ball toward the target. You will get acceleration," Judy insists. "As your swing develops and gets better, you will find that you have a long flat area in your swing. In the midst of that flat area, when the golf ball gets in the way of the clubhead, you strike the back of that golf ball solidly and firmly. You achieve acceleration. You do it by freely swinging the club through the ball to the target, not by trying to hit down hard on the ball."

When you see a player whose swing stops shortly after she hits the ball, that means she tried to maneuver the club instead of swinging it. "A lot of women don't swing the club. They try to maneuver it," Jerilyn Britz observes. "Because a woman is not as strong as a man, you have to allow the momentum of the clubhead to hit the ball. You can learn to do this well with time and practice."

Hollis Stacy thinks of acceleration as swinging hard. Nowadays the average golf pro will take a junior girl and tell her, "Hit the ball. Learn to hit the ball hard. Don't slug the ball." There is a difference between hitting and slugging. When you hit the ball you stay in balance. When you slug the ball you cannot. You fall forward or backward from your shot.

"Probably the biggest fallacy I've been taught is just to swing through," Hollis Stacy reflects. "Now, when I'm showing my sisters how to play, I tell them to swing hard. Get the maximum clubhead speed you can. You'd be surprised, when you get that clubhead speed going, how you start taking the club through straight.

"Clubhead speed is the result of club, arms, shoulders, hips, legs—everything working together. Go ahead and swing with all of your physical motion when you're learning how to swing a golf club. It can become your natural thing. So what if your shots spray all over at first? You will straighten them out once you have the idea of swinging the club hard."

FOLLOW-THROUGH

When you swing freely, follow-through takes place. It is a

basic fact of a good golf swing that when you swing your club completely it finishes over your left shoulder.

You can't create follow-through. Good follow-through is the result of making a good swing. Anyone who tries to direct the club to the ball at impact slows the club down so much that the follow-through can't happen. It only happens when you swing the club freely through the ball.

"Work on the follow-through," admonish the pros. More than one observes, "So many people work on the backswing. They do take the club back beautifully. But then, on their downswing, they tend to hit at the ball. They don't follow through. When you hit at the ball you'll hit the ball. But there's nothing beyond that. There's no momentum to create distance. The minute you quit on a shot, you lose a tremendous amount of distance. You cut it off. When you are following through you finish with your hands high. You finish looking at your target."

Beth Daniel thinks some women worry too much about

Beth Daniel's head comes up naturally, her hips and shoulders rotate, and her arms fly up and over to follow through and complete her swing.

keeping their heads down for a good follow-through. When your head is down your arms can go only so far. Let your head come up naturally as your hips rotate and your arms go to the target. That allows you to follow through.

To finish your swing with a good follow-through, Marlene Floyd reminds you, "Just always make sure the club finishes over your left shoulder. Some women tend to finish out to the right. That means they are trying to extend too much toward the target. Once your club has hit the golf ball, let it swing up and over. The more relaxed you are on your follow-through, the quicker the ball pops up into the air. Remember, to create a good shot, the follow-through is more important than the backswing."

A ROUTINE

"When you set up to hit a golf ball it's a good idea to develop some sort of routine. It helps you hit more of your shots the same way," advises Judy Rankin.

Find a routine that works for you. If you're used to putting your hands on the club before you lay the clubhead down behind the ball, do it that way every time.

In your routine, line up the golf club first. Decide where you want to aim the ball. Then position your feet—the left foot first, then the right one. Waggle a little, put your club up to the ball and take it away again a couple of times if it relaxes you.

Using a routine at setup doesn't mean you have to be a slow player. After a while it's so automatic that it's almost a part of your swing.

STRENGTH

Strength is a factor in making a good golf swing. That can't be ignored. A woman who has had hip surgery or is physically weak cannot hit a golf ball as far as a woman in good physical shape who exercises frequently. But that is one of the pluses of the golf game. Everyone can achieve success within her own capabilities.

You might think the women pros play enough golf to give them all the strength they need. But they still have to exercise to maintain it. Amy Alcott jogs daily, if possible. Judy Rankin faithfully does push-ups in her motel room. All the pros have particular exercises they do regularly.

If your lifestyle limits your exercise, especially during the winter months, consider starting some sort of exercise routine in the spring to limber up for the golf season. If you are seriously trying to develop your game, exercise should be part of your golf program.

YOU AND YOUR SWING

Work on all the aspects of the basic swing. On a practice range or at an indoor range, practice at your own pace. How quickly you acquire the skills and master the swing well enough to go out onto the course to play depends on you and the time you have to spend.

The important thing is to make your practice time count.

Picture the overall swing in your mind. Look at these pictures of the pros illustrating particular basics. Try to imitate them. Apply the fundamentals of the basic swing to develop a swing of your own. If you can, occasionally have a pro check your progress.

Here's a summary of the basics you want to work on:

1. **Grip.** Grip the club with your left hand. Keep the thumb to the right of center, straight down the shaft, holding the club firmly with the last three fingers. Place your right hand directly below the left. Bend your fingers around the club with the pinkie alongside the index finger of the left hand and the middle finger on the left side of the center of the shaft.

2. **Stance.** Stand with your feet about shoulder width apart, square with the ball. Bend slightly at the waist, flex your knees, and bend your head slightly.

3. **Ball Position.** Place the ball off your left heel.

4. **Alignment.** Put your clubface square to the ball on the line of flight to the target. Make sure your feet are parallel to that line.

5. **Hands and Arms.** Address the ball with your hands slightly ahead of the ball, your left arm in a straight line with the shaft down to the clubhead. Bend your right arm slightly in toward your body. Keep your grip firm, your arms relaxed.

6. **Footwork.** Shift your weight from the left heel to the right heel as you take the club back, then from the right heel to the left as you swing the club forward.

7. **Rhythm and Tempo.** Time your flow of movement as you take your club back to the top of your backswing, pause, then come downward, extending your club through the ball and up over your left shoulder to finish the swing.

8. **Acceleration.** Develop clubhead speed with your club, arms, shoulder, hips—everything—working together, going through the ball.

9. **Follow-through.** Hit through the ball toward the target and finish with hands high, your club up and over your left shoulder, to complete your swing.

3

The Medium Irons

"As a beginner, you have to learn a few good techniques about swinging a golf club initially," says Marlene Floyd. To enjoy learning, Marlene recommends, "Take lessons, read good books on golf, watch good players play, and start out with your medium irons."

The medium irons are the most valuable clubs in a beginner's bag. Use them to learn how to swing a golf club. Marlene and many pros recommend that you begin swinging with your seven iron.

Go to the practice range, tee the ball up, and learn to get it airborne. Develop your tempo with the ball on the tee. When you get all the balls flying off the tee, then put the ball down on the ground. When you can consistently hit all the balls solidly with the seven iron, switch to the five iron.

"Hit down and through the ball, not up on it," Marlene emphasizes. "With the ball on the tee, you shouldn't be scared of the ground, afraid of hurting yourself if you hit it instead of the ball."

The five iron is a good average club. Its face doesn't have too much loft, nor is it too straight. The shaft is a good length. When you can hit the five iron well, you can walk onto any course to play, confident that you can hit the ball a good distance. You will improve your game with time and practice.

If you start topping the balls or hitting them fat (hitting the ground in front of the ball), put the ball back up on the tee again until you learn to hit the ball first.

HITTING WELL

How do you hit a seven, six, or five iron consistently well?

"Right from the start, imprint on your mind that you should let the clubhead do the work," says Marlene. "The loft of the clubface was designed to send the ball flying into the air at impact. And it will, if you don't try to help it by trying to scoop or power the ball up. The clubhead does its work when you swing freely through the ball."

Marlene's basics for hitting good medium iron shots are to learn the grip, the stance, alignment, footwork, and follow-through. Other players will stress other fundamentals. These are Marlene's.

She recommends the basic overlap grip. Hold the club firmly with the last three fingers of your left hand. Put your right hand below the left, bringing your pinkie to rest nestled between the index and middle finger of your left hand. This keeps both your hands working together. For details, see Chapter 2.

"Take your stance a bit narrower than shoulder width and slightly open," she advises. "Position the ball just a little forward of center, not quite as far as the left heel."

Some pros play every iron with the ball in that position. Others move the ball back a little in their stance for each progressively lower iron, to be able to hit down on the ball easier. This is something you can work out for yourself on the practice range. You might find that playing the ball back

Using an overlap grip, Marlene Floyd positions her hands slightly ahead of the ball to play the medium irons. Her stance is a bit narrower and slightly open. Her left arm and the club shaft form a straight line to the clubhead, placed square with the ball. She plays the ball just off her left heel.

slightly in your stance gives you solid ball contact more consistently.

With your hands slightly ahead of the ball, your left arm and the club shaft are in a straight line. Your arms fall into place normally.

ALIGNMENT

Alignment determines where your ball goes when you hit it.

"Line up your clubface square to the ball and to your target. This line between the clubface and target is called the line of target," Marlene explains. "Then line up your feet, your body, and your shoulders parallel to that line. That is how you align your swing."

When you line up your body, rather than your ball, to the target, the ball will land to the right of where you want it.

If you have difficulty figuring out alignment, check it out on the practice range. Lay a club down along an imaginary line from your ball to the target. Then lay down another club in front of your feet, parallel to the ball-to-target line. If you are aligned correctly, the clubs should look like a railroad track.

FOOTWORK

"Think about a baseball swing. That's the way a golf club swings," says Marlene. "It's a rotating movement. The more relaxed you are in the arms, the quicker the ball will pop into the air. I have a firm grip but relaxed arms when I address the ball."

Footwork comes into focus when you start to take your club back from the ball to make your backswing.

"As you take the club back, your weight should shift from the middle part of your left foot to your right heel—not to the outside of your right foot," Marlene says. "Your left knee will be bent slightly inward. When you pause at the top of the backswing to let the club change direction and set your hands, your weight should be completely off the left foot."

Below, left: As Marlene takes her iron back, her footwork initiates the shift of her weight from the middle part of her left foot to her right foot. Below, right: At the top of her backswing, Marlene has completed her weight shift from her left foot to her right. Her left knee is bent slightly inward, her left heel lifted slightly off the ground.

She goes on to describe the footwork of a swing. "As your shoulder and body turn around, your weight returns to the left heel. As you swing the club down, your weight is firmly on the outside of your left heel. Learn the proper footwork of the swing and 90 percent of the time you will be in a perfect swing pattern.

Above, left: As her downswing begins, you see Marlene's weight shifting back to her left foot. Her left heel is back on the ground. Her left knee is in a forward position. Above, right: Marlene's weight is on the outside of her left foot as she extends through her swing. Her right heel has lifted up off the ground, following her weight shift.

"Don't try to keep a straight left arm consciously as you bring your club back," Marlene adds. "That's too difficult. If you just turn your arms and your shoulders to bring the club back, up and over your right shoulder, your arm will automatically be straight."

She emphasizes, "The key to a successful medium iron shot is to hit down against the ball and through the hitting area. If your wrists break at impact, you get a scooping or flipping action. You hit the ball thin or fat."

FOLLOW-THROUGH

Finish high with the club over your left shoulder. Concentrate on follow-through. Many women tend to finish their swing out to the right. "That means you are trying to extend down the line too much to keep the club going at the target," analyzes Marlene. "Once the club hits the golf ball it should swing up and over your left shoulder. When you try to hold your swing down you tend to block the shot."

Marlene believes golf is a game of mental images. "Keep a picture of the follow-through in your head. If you get a picture in your mind of what you want to do, and you understand it, then your body will do it. Watching good players swing is a good way to form those mental pictures."

Visualize this follow-through to imitate. Marlene's weight shift is completed. Only the toe of her right foot touches the ground. Her weight rests on the outside of her left foot, back on her heel.

DEVELOPING SKILLS

As your skill with the medium irons grows, so will the confidence you feel in using them. You'll discover a multitude of ways to use them.

You can, for example, count on your five iron for 110- to 115-yard shots when your swing is developed. The five iron is a good club to use when you have to hit into the wind or anytime you need a club with a little loft and not too straight a face.

You can use your five, six, or seven iron around the green for chip or finesse shots. When you're in trouble in the rough or in a fairway bunker, pull one out of your bag. You developed your swing with these clubs, and they won't fail you.

These irons also make excellent warm-up clubs. Use them before you start playing. Finally, turn to the five, six, or seven iron when you want to hit a fade shot (to the right) or draw (to the left) into a green.

"Golf is almost a game of opposites," Marlene notes. "To make the ball go right, you hit left. To go left, you aim right. It's your body that can change the line.

"When you want your ball to go to the right (fade), aim your body about 10 degrees left of the target. Put the ball forward in your stance and aim the ball and clubface toward the target. With your body, feet, and hips aimed left, and your clubface aimed directly at the target, you swing down across your body line (the line where your body is aimed) in an outside-in direction. Your ball fades as it flies.

"When you want your ball to go left, aim your body about 10 degrees to the right of the target. Put the ball back in your stance and aim the ball and clubface at the target. With this stance you will swing across your body line in an inside-out direction. Your ball draws as it flies."

You always swing along your body line to hook or slice a shot. But you still aim your clubface and ball at the target. That's why it's necessary to understand the idea of alignment from the very beginning, when you are learning how to swing.

KEEP YOUR SWING

"To this day, when I find myself not hitting well I go back on the practice range and hit my irons off a tee," Marlene reveals. "I have a perfect lie then. The ball is going to come up. Then, after I get some confidence I put the ball back down on the ground.

"Try it yourself when you find you are having trouble hitting any of your clubs—not getting your ball up in the air."

Your medium irons can become the most reliable clubs in your bag. Master Marlene's fundamentals for swinging them.

1. Grip your club wih a basic overlap grip, holding the club firmly with the last three fingers of your left hand. The right hand is below the left, its pinkie connecting your hands.

2. Take a stance a bit narrower than shoulder width and slightly open, with the ball slightly forward.

3. Line up your clubface square with the ball and the target; your feet should be square with the line of flight.

4. Address the ball with your hands slightly forward, your left arm and the club shaft in a straight line, your hands firm, arms relaxed.

5. Develop footwork. Shift your weight from your left heel to your right as you bring the club back. Bend your left knee slightly inward, with the weight completely off the left foot at the top of the backswing. As you turn your body and shoulders, your weight returns to the left heel. Swing down with your weight firmly on the outside of the left heel.

6. Follow through, finishing high with the club over your left shoulder.

7. Practice on the practice range with the ball teed up until you are consistently hitting a solid shot.

4
The Woods

Master the fairway woods and you are on your way to good times on the golf course. True, holing a putt is exciting. But flying a ball high and true, 150 yards or so down the fairway time after time is fun. It's exhilarating.

It takes patience and practice to learn to hit the woods well. But once you start playing the game you'll find you're pulling a wood out of your bag to use at least once or twice on every hole. The sooner you become good at hitting one, the quicker your game will devleop.

"I suggest that when you begin learning how to hit the fairway woods you put the ball up on a tee at the practice range, just as you did to learn to hit the irons," says Myra Van Hoose. "That gives you the feeling of swinging the club to get the ball airborne, instead of trying to help the ball up or being afraid to strike at it solidly for fear of hitting the ground. Right from the start, you want to make solid contact with the ball."

The three and four woods are usually referred to as the fairway woods. The five wood has more loft. It is the club most beginners find the easiest to use to learn how to hit woods. After you can hit a five wood solidly you can try the four wood, then the three wood.

Once you do hit your woods consistently, you can expect to get about 130 yards with the five wood, 140 with the four wood and 150 yards with the three wood. Of course, those yardages are averages only; actual yardages will vary with how hard you swing your club and the other conditions of play.

ADDRESS

Address the fairway woods as you do most of your other clubs. Position the ball just inside of, or off, your left heel.

As instructed in Chapter 2, grip the club firmly with the last three fingers of your left hand, placing the thumb just to the right of the center of the shaft. The V formed between your forefinger and the thumb should aim at your right shoulder. Wrap your right index finger and thumb around the shaft, resting the pinkie alongside the index finger of the left hand and the middle finger.

To play a fairway wood, Myra Van Hoose holds the club firmly with the last three fingers of her left hand, using her right hand to steady it. Her stance is shoulder-wide, square to the ball, with her weight slightly back on her heels. She holds her left arm straight, her right arm in toward her body. Her hands are slightly ahead of the ball, her arms relaxed. She bends her body slightly at the waist with her head down a little and her knees flexed.

Don't let that V open up on your left hand. Be sure you can see two knuckles of your left hand as you grip the club. Your right hand acts as a steadying support. You don't have to grip tightly with it. Relax your arms as you grip the club firmly but not tensely.

Position your feet about shoulder width apart, with your weight evenly distributed, slightly favoring your heels. Bend at your waist slightly and flex your knees a little. Make sure your left arm and the club shaft form a straight line to the clubhead. Square your clubface to the target.

"Alignment is very important, giving you a much better chance to put the ball where you want it," emphasizes Myra. "Line up your clubhead to the target. Then your body will be parallel to that line."

Golfers frequently hear the instruction, "Keep your eye on the ball." But don't let that rule cause you to put your head down so diligently that you can't take the club back. You need to be able to turn your shoulders around as you take your club back. If your head is down too far, your shoulders can't turn freely because your head is in the way.

BACKSWING

Keep your right elbow tucked in to limit your backswing. Myra explains, "If you let your elbow fly, the clubhead can get too high. Keeping your right elbow tucked in limits your swing. You can't overswing. It keeps your swing where it should be."

Tempo is the key of a good wood swing—actually, of any golf swing. Take your wood back easily and slowly. Sweep it back as you slowly turn your hips and shoulders. Gradually shift your weight from your left to your right foot.

"As I take the club back, my right knee stays in the same position," says Myra, describing her swing. "I turn at the waist, keeping my right elbow tucked in."

Keep your left arm straight, though not rigid, as you swing back. Don't let it collapse. Take the club back far enough to give you a reasonably long downswing.

Above, left: Myra takes the club away with a slow sweeping motion. Her head remains steady, her right elbow tucked in close to her body. She keeps her left arm straight as it follows her shoulder turn. Above, right: As Myra turns, her body and shoulders rotate to bring her arms up with the club. Her weight shift from left to right is reflected in her left knee bending inward. But she does not roll her left foot or lift her heel, as happens with many other players, to more positively initiate weight shift from left to right.

At the top of her backswing, Myra's right leg is braced; her weight is on her right foot. As she sets her hands, her grip remains firm. Her left arm is reasonably straight. Her back is to the target.

"I set my hands at the top of my backswing," notes Myra. "My back is to the target." She reminds you to keep your grip firm at the top of the backswing and your left arm reasonably straight. That helps to give you a good swing arc and forces your muscles to stretch.

DOWNSWING

"Come down, making sure to extend through the ball," Myra directs. "Be conscious of your left arm and left hand moving toward the target as you make solid contact with the ball."

Swing hard through the ball to get maximum clubhead speed. Remember that this speed comes from your club, arms, shoulders, hips, legs, and feet, all working together.

Lead into the downswing with your lower body. As your hips turn, your weight shifts back to your left foot. Your

Below, left: On her downswing, Myra consciously leads with her lower body. As her hips turn, her weight shifts back to her left. Below, right: As Myra swings, her hips turn, and her shoulders and arms follow, pulling the club. She says she tries to get a feeling of turning her hips as she swings down.

shoulder and arms follow, pulling the club. Try to get a feeling of turning your hips as you swing back down. Extend your left arm and hand toward the target. Complete your follow-through, up and over your left shoulder.

You might not be able to analyze the part of a pro's swing that reveals her extending toward the hole or shows her hips turning. But in picture after picture you can see examples of a complete follow-through. You can see what you should imitate in your swing.

The follow-through is a result of your swing. You can't create it. It just happens when you really let your club go.

Below, left: Extend. This is one of Myra's key words. You see it here in her swing. She is extending her club through the ball toward the target after impact for maximum distance and strong follow-through. Below, right: All of the energy Myra put into extending in her swing is reflected in her body here. She really lets her club go and swings. Her follow-through is complete as she faces the target.

KEY WORDS

"I only think about three things when I swing," reveals Myra. "Keep the right knee braced. Keep my right elbow tucked in. Extend. That's the basis of my whole swing."

"I can realistically say that when I'm playing I can only think of two things to remind myself to do in my swing," Sally Little reflects. "Golf is hard enough without having ten different thoughts when you are trying to make your swing. My keys are words, like *stretch* or *hard*. They change as different problems arise."

Using key phrases or words to help maintain a consistent swing is an excellent pro trick to imitate. Like Myra, you can repeat the basics of your swing to yourself: "Bring left shoulder under. Pause at the top. Come through hard." Or, like Sally, you can try key words—*slow* and *firm*, which, for example—you change from round to round.

Whatever choice you make, the idea is to keep your swing thoughts simple. Overthinking when you're out on the course can ruin a good swing. Work your problems out on the practice range.

HITTING DOWN

Perhaps you've heard, via verbal advice or the written word, that you should hit down on the golf ball as you swing. Judy Rankin takes exception to such instruction, especially for beginning golfers. "Taking a divot is not done by striking down on a golf ball. If you literally struck down on a golf ball, you would top it every time you hit it. You take a divot because you are swinging through the ball, toward the target. If your swing happens to be pretty good, you're going to hit the ground. But you're not striking down on the ground. You are going through the ground. It's a completely different thing.

"The term *striking down* destroys many amateur golfers. Anybody who tries to strike down naturally swings across the ball. That's the only way you can go.

"The best golfers have what we call a long flat area in their swing. In the midst of that flat area the golf ball gets in the way of the clubhead. You sweep along the terrain rather than down into the terrain. You cannot strike the back of the golf ball if you strike down on the ball.

"Swing the club through the ball to the target. Try to strike the back side of the golf ball, the side opposite the target, to hit the ball solidly," Judy emphasizes.

You can see this flat area in Judy Rankin's swing as her club sweeps along to strike the ball at the greatest clubhead speed. You see, she does not strike down on the ball. She sweeps through the ball.

This photo illustrates how Judy continues to swing her club freely toward the target after her clubhead has struck the back side of the ball solidly at impact.

DISTANCE

Women golfers cannot hit the ball very far, using only their arms and hands, as a lot of men are able to do. Most women don't have that kind of strength.

Become conscious of shifting your weight from your left foot to your right, rolling the weight off your left foot as you take your backswing. Your weight should be completely off your left foot by the time you are at the top of your backswing. Then you must bring it back to your left foot as you come forward on your downswing. You should actually lift your right heel off the ground as you follow through.

That kind of footwork will improve your clubhead contact at impact. You'll see your balls flying farther down the fairways.

If you never achieve much distance, but you are holding your game together, Nancy Lopez has encouraging advice for you.

"Women are always asking me, 'How can I get more distance?' Many women just don't hit the ball real far. But distance is not that important. If you can practice well enough to know just how far you do hit each of your clubs, that's what counts. If it takes you a wood to get on the green, and your playing partner uses a five iron, what's the difference? Make your game your own game."

Don't become frustrated by the limitations of your ability and become too serious, too intense about the game. Nancy feels the first reason for amateurs to play golf is to relax and have a good time playing the game. A woman who has had hip surgery can't aspire to the same game as a woman who has been active and agile all her life. But she can hit steady shots down the fairway and deadly ones around the green, if she practices.

INCREASING DISTANCE

If you have a good, consistent swing and are looking for a way to get more distance with your fairway woods, Myra suggests that you put more decided leg action into your swing. She has an exercise to help you learn how to do this.

"Take your club to the top of the backswing and stop. Then come down consciously, with your legs leading. Take the club back, brace your right knee, and keep it in position. From the top of the backswing, first move your legs through the ball; then your arms follow. You are not moving your arms consciously; rather, your legs move your arms.

Here Myra demonstrates her exercise to put more leg action into the swing to get more distance. She emphasizes keeping your right leg braced as you bring back your club to the top of your backswing.

Here Myra shows the lateral thrust left as her lower body pushes off her braced right leg. She feels this is the key of the movement. Her hips rotate. Her legs lead her shoulders and arms. She consciously shifts her weight with her legs first, trying to keep her upper body behind so her club will be behind the ball at impact.

If you can time your lower body to shift forward, leading your shoulders and arms, as you see Myra do here, you will come through impact behind the ball. This movement takes practice. It is a coordination of rhythm and timing with body movement.

"It's kind of like your legs make a lateral move toward the target that leads your arms down, so you come through extending. The turn of your waist and hips causes the club to come through squarely. You are not moving your hands at all to do this. Your legs initiate the downswing."

From the photos in this book you can see this lateral move being done by many of the pros. Try to imitate it as you see it. Or talk to your pro in more detail about how you might insert that kind of move into your swing.

LOFTED OR UTILITY WOODS

"Start using the lofted woods, the five and the seven, regularly in your game. You'll be a better player," declares Sally Little. "I believe only women with handicaps of nine and under (scores in the low 80s) should ever use a two iron. It is such a difficult club to use. Anyone over a 16 handicap (scores around 90) shouldn't be using a three iron. I really don't believe they should. It's such a difficult club to use. Pitch out the three iron. Put in a seven wood. Nowadays there are five woods and seven woods that play just as well as the long irons for an average player.

"You can hit a seven wood out of the long rough. You can hit it off a tee. There are a lot of women on our tour and also on the men's tour who are starting to use these clubs. Why not? They can hit them farther and better."

In addition to the five and seven woods, many manufacturers also offer utility or trouble woods. They are given special names, such as Ginty, Rambler, and Scrambler, by the manufacturers. The loft of these woods allows you to hit them high. They also are made with a special flange on the bottom of the club to help get the ball up into the air more easily. Experiment with one to see what it can do for you.

Nancy Lopez recommends that, for the ideal golf set, the average woman would have five woods—the driver, a three, five, and seven wood, plus a utility wood.

"You don't have to work as hard to hit a shot off a bare lie or out of very heavy rough using a good utility club," Amy Alcott declares. "Psychologically, every man and woman should have a lofted wood, such as a six or seven. It's an advantage. The loft of the wood gives you a lot of advantage."

Off a bare spot, you can hit the ball first by using a utility wood. The loft of that club will put the ball up and put a backspin on it.

"Playing with lofted woods is the better way for most women who play for fun," Judy Rankin adds. "When you add a seven or utility wood to your bag, you can hit the ball higher. It will drop a little softer on the green, and hold better.

"You need lofted woods to get out of the rough. I use a two iron and a five wood. In high rough I almost always take my five wood. I'm strong as female golfers go. But I'm much better out of long grass with a wood than I am with an iron. I want to get out of the rough and still get some distance. So I go with a lofted wood."

When you need a relatively long shot from a moderate rough, play the ball in the middle of your stance. Take a square stance and align your body parallel to the line of flight with your hands slightly ahead of the ball. Aim the clubface slightly to the right of the target because the grass may interfere with it, causing the clubface to close at impact. You can expect a lower, longer-running shot.

These utility woods are made especially to get the ball up and out of a rough and put overspin on it to get some distance.

Anytime you have to hit a ball out of the rough, you can expect the ball to roll farther on the green or on the fairway and to be deflected to a certain degree. That's just what hitting from the rough does to a ball. Using a lofted wood does limit that bounce and roll more than an iron would. But most important, when you take a lofted wood in hand, it's going to be easier to hit your ball up and out of trouble.

Should you swing the utility woods or the five or seven woods any differently than other fairway woods? Basically, no.

"I do take a much smoother swing with my seven wood than with my three wood," reflects Myra. "I use the three wood for distance alone. I use the seven wood for a lot of purposes. It is my utility club, my stroke saver, more or less.

"For me, a smoother swing means a slower swing. My tempo is slower than for a three wood or a driver, where I'm trying for maximum clubhead speed and distance. With my seven wood I want loft and accuracy."

So, what does Myra advise about a seven wood shot? "Play the ball back in your stance more. Try a slow tempo swing. Choke down on the club a little, if you feel that gives you more control. Other than that, swing it as you do any other wood."

KNOW-HOW

Woods can become the stalwarts of your game. With concentration, patience, and practice, you can learn to hit them so well that you will simply love to play golf. The basics of a good wood shot will come automatically to you.

1. Grip the club properly, as instructed in Chapter 2.
2. Stand with your feet shoulder width apart, your weight evenly distributed, somewhat concentrated on your heels.
3. Bend slightly at your waist, flex your knees, and bend your head only slightly.
4. Form a straight line with your left arm and the club shaft down to the clubface. Bend your right arm in toward your body. Your grip should be firm, your arms relaxed.
5. Position the ball just inside of your left heel. Square the clubface to the target and the ball.
6. Take your club back, sweeping it slowly, keeping your left arm straight. Shift your weight from your left to your right foot as you turn your hips and shoulders to bring the club back far enough to allow room to make a good downswing.

Unless your grip is correct, your swing cannot be effective. Sally Little has a perfect overlap grip here. Study it. Hold the picture in front of you to grip your club the same way.

Sally plays her ball farther back in her stance for a shot from the rough. You would move it forward slightly on the fairway. You can imitate her stance to address your ball. Copy the position of her body, head, arms, hands, and legs. This is the way you want to address your ball.

Sweep your club back from the ball as Sally does. Don't be in a hurry to lift it up, breaking your left arm, letting your right arm fly.

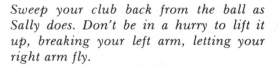

7. At the top of the backswing, pause to set your wrists. Start your weight shift back to your left.

8. Begin your downswing with your lower body, hips turning, your arms following.

You know your backswing is far enough to allow you room for a good downswing when your shoulder is under your chin like Sally's is. Her weight has shifted completely from her left to her right side. Do that. Then pause to set yourself as Sally does.

Here Sally shows how she starts her weight shift back from her right to her left side as soon as she starts her downswing.

9. Come through the ball at the peak of clubhead speed, extending your left arm and hand toward the target.

As her weight goes forward to her left foot, Sally turns her hips and shoulders to bring her arms down, leading her clubhead. Try keeping your left arm straight as she does to achieve a swing arc like hers.

This is a picture that shows what extending through the ball means. You don't have to explain it, but you can imitate it.

10. Complete your follow-through, bringing the club up and over your left shoulder.

When your follow-through looks like Sally's you know you've hit a terrific wood shot.

5

The Short Game

The short shots are the best part of Amy Alcott's game. She'll tell you, "There never was a good chipper who didn't have good feel.

"The shots around the green—the short game—can become the best part of any woman's game," Amy says fervently. "It calls for the kind of accuracy you develop from the natural feel in your hands. You don't need power to sharpen your short game, just determination to go for the pin every time."

The short game includes all those shots you need to put your ball as close as possible to the pin from 50 yards on into the green. They don't call for a regular full swing. Some are termed *pitch shots*, others *chip shots*. They're also known as *par savers* and *birdie makers*. Any of these can be the coup de maître of your game.

Or, as Jerilyn Britz says, "You can make up for a lot of mistakes out on the fairway, if you develop confidence and a good technique around the green."

PITCH OR CHIP

A pitch shot is the longer shot. It puts more carry (loft) on the ball, less roll. If you are anywhere from 20 feet out and want to hit your ball high to the green to land with a minimum of roll, you use a pitch shot. You want the ball to bite the green when it lands, stopping as quickly as possible. Those are the kinds of shots you have to hit to get over bunkers or water in front of a green.

A chip shot calls for more roll, less loft on the ball. When you are around the outskirts of the green or on the apron (that fringe of grass around a green), and you want to hit a little shot that will just carry over a few feet or a few inches of turf to land on the green and then roll to the pin, you use a chip shot.

Both pitching and chipping involve visualizing where you want the ball to land on the green so it can roll to the pin. The spot you choose to aim for depends on the angle of the green, how fast or slow the green is, where your ball lies on the fairway, and what kind of a lie it has. Amy calls these "the finesse shots of the golf game."

Whether it's a long nine iron pitch from 50 feet or a little 10-foot chip with a pitching wedge, it takes finesse to put that ball just where you want it on the green to roll to the cup.

THE PITCH

Take an open stance to make a pitch shot. Keep your weight on your left foot, which should be placed back from your intended line of flight, back from your right foot. Keep your feet close together and stand closer to the ball than you do for a full-swing, short iron shot. Play the ball slightly off your left foot, just a few inches from the left heel. As you address the ball, keep your hands ahead of the clubhead.

"The key to a good short shot is keeping a firm left wrist," emphasizes Amy. "There should be no break in the left wrist as you swing the club. The minute the left wrist turns over

Amy Alcott just hit a solid short shot. Her shoulders have turned and her knees are bent forward a little from her open stance. Her head remains down. Notice her right elbow close to her side. Her club has come through slightly open. The loft of the ball reflects her firm hand action at impact—no break in her left wrist. The back of her left hand remains directed to the hole.

(turns left) or quits (turns right), you lose your accuracy. Think about hitting the ball solidly, hitting the ball first, hitting the ball crisply. Finish up with the back of your left hand toward the hole."

Hitting the ball first puts the backspin on the ball that you need to control the pitch. Hold the club firmly in your left hand. As you take your backswing, use a full shoulder turn, but little body movement. Keep your heels on the ground but let your knees bend forward.

Swing smoothly, rhythmically, keeping your right elbow close to your side. As your clubface comes through slightly open, use a firm hand action to uncock your wrist at impact and loft the ball as you swing through to the pin.

You can use a seven, eight, or nine iron or a pitching wedge for these pitch shots. Your choice depends on the distance you need.

If you try to scoop the ball up with the loft of the club or happen to close or hood the clubface as you come through the ball, you'll miss the shot. The same is true if you take a long backswing, then baby the shot coming through.

When you have to hit a pitch shot from the rough, adjust your clubface a little. Open it more to address the ball; that is, turn the toe of the clubhead slightly to the right. Rough has a tendency to close the clubhead on contact. Be sure that your left hand stays firm and you hit the shot harder than you would from the same distance on the fairway.

THE CHIP

The basic stance for a chip shot is also slightly open but narrower than for a pitch shot. Feel your weight on your left side from your hips down through your knee to your foot. Play the ball back off your left heel.

For these shots close to the green, some golfers feel more control if they grip the club farther down than normally. You can bend more at the waist for this shot. Do whatever is comfortable for you.

"The key to good chipping is to keep your left wrist firm," stresses Amy. "There should be no break in your left wrist as you swing the club back. But how far back you take the club depends solely on how far you have to hit the ball. Swing smoothly, firmly."

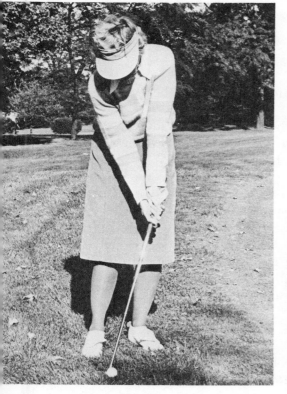

*Take a narrow, slightly open
stance, with your weight on
your left side for a chip shot.
Position the ball back off
your left foot. Keeping your
left arm straight, your right
arm close to your body,
stand close to the ball. Be
certain your hands are ahead
of it. Bend over as much as
feels comfortable to you.*

*As you take the club back, keep
the clubface square to the ball
and your left wrist firm. Think
about hitting the ball first,
crisply. How far you take the
club back depends on how far
you have to hit the ball.*

As you take the club back, try to keep the clubface square with the ball.

"Think about hitting the ball solidly," advises Amy. "Hit the ball first, and hit it crisply. Finish up with the backside of your left hand right at the hole."

Emphasizing her directions, she adds, "Come through the ball. Don't swing at the ball. Chipping is like putting. You must come through the ball. Keep the back of your left hand going to the pin. The minute your left wrist turns over or quits, you lose accuracy."

Irons used for chipping range from the four up to the sand wedge. The choice is usually determined by the amount of roll you want as well as the distance you need.

FEEL

"Chipping is feel. A lot of it can't be taught." Amy elaborates: "If you have a shot to the pin 30 feet from the edge and you are chipping with an iron from just off the green, there's no one who can tell you how far to take your club back or how hard to hit the ball. You have to feel that for yourself. You have to work to develop your own feel."

To chip well, you have to feel what you want to accomplish and be able to see what you have to do. You have to feel how hard you have to hit the ball out of the rough to make it land on the spot you have targeted on the green, where it should land in order to roll to the hole.

Amy Alcott shows good form after hitting the ball—her head is down and her hands are toward the pin.

"Some people are clumsy with their hands," Amy observes, "so they have to work a lot harder at the short game to become proficient. Others have a natural feel for how hard to hit a ball, from all sorts of different lies, to carry it to the green. Experiment with what works best for you."

Sandra Palmer shares similar thoughts about the short game. "After you have your basic swing down for your short game, spend a lot of time chipping around the greens. It kind of gives you that touch. Touch to me means *stopping the ball at the hole.* It's better not to think too technically just how you're going to do it. Just work on a touch. That's the short game."

EXPERIMENT

"Never feel inhibited to experiment with different shots," encourages Amy. "You can start chipping little shots around the green with a pitching wedge and a sand wedge. These won't give you much roll. Then try using a seven iron to see what the difference in the loft does to the roll the ball has.

A wedge shot to the green gives you loft, not much roll.

"If you have more green to work with, like a 30-foot roll, why not use a six, seven, or eight iron? I firmly believe that when you have a lot of green to work with, like 30, 40, 50 feet, the lower you can keep the ball to the ground, the more accurate your chip is going to be. A lot of people feel they must lift the ball in the air on a shot like that. I disagree. That might look better. But it is more effective to keep your ball low to the ground."

To make such shots work for you, you have to practice them. Amy warns, "Never stick to a wedge just because you have good results with it. True, there are certain shots you will always use a wedge to hit. But don't be afraid to work with different clubs to see which work best for other shots. Don't be afraid to become proficient."

When you have more green to work with, hit a seven iron low to the ground. Just carry it over the turf to roll to the cup.

Practice in your backyard or in the park or at an indoor range. Pick different targets and try different clubs to reach them. That kind of practice helps sharpen perspective and gives you a picture of how far each club hits the ball and how high the ball goes. You'll learn to judge how much backswing you need to hit the ball a certain distance. An hour or two of practice for one evening every week can markedly improve your pitching and chipping.

"Be patient. Acquiring finesse takes time," says Amy. "Everyone wants it right now. But realize that you're not going to get it in a day or maybe in a year. But, if you can find the time to work at it, you will see yourself improving."

KNOW-HOW

As you become a better player, you will find more and more that you wish you had special know-how to help you make some particularly unusual, challenging shot. It does take know-how to hit these well.

You don't always have to use your short irons or wedges to make the shots around the green. "Try using your putter from just off the green when the grass is thin or very short. You don't have to chip. You can run the ball onto the green. Always play the percentage shot, not the fancy, more daring one," advises Amy.

"If the grass is heavier and you have a lot of green to work with, use a club similar to a putter, like a three or four iron. Grip the club, holding it slightly ahead (left) of the clubhead. Then hit the ball as you would with a putter. The weight of the clubhead will get the ball through the grass, and hitting it like a putter will roll the ball for you."

When your ball sits on bare ground near the green, the safest kind of shot to make is with a putter. But if the ball is on a bare spot with a hill or such in front of it, you have to use a heavier club to get over the turf. Try a more lofted club, an eight, a nine, or a wedge. Move the grip of the club forward and play the ball two or three inches back in your stance. That thwarts the tendency everyone has to try to scoop

Jerilyn Britz opens her stance and plays the ball back when she uses her putter from the longer grass off the green. Notice that her hands are well ahead of the ball. She has hooded the clubface slightly.

the ball up. Holding the club this way, you can hit the ball first with a descending blow using a shorter stroke.

To play the ball from different types of lies around the green takes skill and practice—and a lot of finesse, Amy would add.

When your ball is in the heavy rough, deep down, Amy plays a cut shot. To get the ball out, she "knocks the props out from under it." That takes skill. You have to smack the ball up right away, popping it out of the rough. To do this, use your sand wedge. Open your stance more than you would otherwise do. Take the club away slightly on the outside. Swing down, leading the club firmly with your left hand. Actually, you kind of cut under the ball. You don't try to follow through. You can't. How hard you hit and how far back you take the club, depend on how far the ball has to go. But to get it out of that deep rough, you must make a firm, deliberate shot.

When the ball is sitting up on fluffy grass or pine needles,

This photo shows that when you "knock the props out from under the ball" buried in heavy rough, you can't follow through. A firm, deliberate swing to cut under the ball stops right where you aim it.

again, play the ball back in your stance. But for this shot, use your least lofted club, like a three or four iron. Hit the ball with a putter-like stroke, keeping your weight on your left foot, to get the ball off its nest.

Pull a five or seven iron out of your bag when you're looking at a downhill chip. All you want to do is try to roll the ball onto the green so it can roll itself down the slope. Choking down a little on the shaft gives you more control.

When you have to hit the ball with some loft to land on a downhill green, use less club than you normally would. For instance, if you would ordinarily use a nine iron, use a wedge to make the shot. You just want to drop the ball onto the green.

This little shot with a lofted club landed just on the downhill green, so it could roll on down. This is what Amy refers to as a finesse shot—takes lots of feel.

When you have to chip up to a pin up on the top of a two-level green, roll the ball up with your regular long chipping club. Don't try a wedge shot to the upper level.

When you are chipping uphill, play the ball off your right foot with your weight forward. That lets you hit the ball as solidly as possible. Use more club than you would for the same distance from a level lie, such as a seven iron instead of an eight.

A lob shot is the most delicate of the short game shots. You use it to clear a bunker, a mound, or water just between you and the green. You want the ball to land on the green with as little roll as possible—to play the ball high or with plenty of loft so the ball will bite the green and hold.

Generally, you would use a wedge, either the sand or the pitching wedge, depending on the distance you have to carry the ball. With your weight on the left foot and the ball off

You open your clubface slightly to lob the ball over sand or water in front of a green. With your weight on your left, bring your pitching or sand wedge down, leading with your left hand. You must break your wrist at impact to get the ball up quickly with backspin to hold the green.

your left heel, bring the club down, leading with your left hand. But break your wrist at impact to get the ball in the air quickly with a backspin to hold the green. This shot is difficult because it calls for more wrist action than other shots. You need practice to master it.

PROBLEMS

Any shot you play for the short game demands that you stay down with the ball. That means you cannot peek to see where the ball is going. If your head comes up, your arms can't follow through to the target.

It's common for women to pull their shots to the green; in other words, the ball lands to the left of the green instead of on it. That usually happens because you are standing too far from your ball or bending at the waist so much that you can't make a free swing.

When you scoop the ball instead of hitting it your weight is on your right instead of your left foot. Let the loft of the club hit the short shot. It can do so when your weight is on your left foot and you're able to hit through the ball.

When you pull out an iron or a wedge to pitch or chip a shot to the green, remember these pointers.

1. Your stance is slightly open, narrower, with your weight decidedly on the left foot.

2. The ball is positioned slightly off your left foot.

3. You stand closer to the ball for chip shots than for pitch shots.

4. Your hands are slightly ahead of the ball.

5. You must keep your left wrist firm as you swing the club. Do not allow it to turn.

6. How far back you take the club and how hard you hit the ball depends on the distance you need.

7. Hit the ball first. Hit it crisply.

8. Finish your swing with the backside of your left hand right at the hole.

6
The Short Irons

When you want to nestle your ball up to the pin anywhere from 80 or 90 yards away or closer, pull a short iron out of your bag. The eight, the nine, or the pitching wedge is the club to do the job. Many a time, a well-placed short iron shot saves par or even gives you a chance for a birdie.

Both how far the club hits the ball and the degree of loft (height) it puts on a ball vary for each short iron.

LOFT

The loft on these short irons is an important factor when you are choosing which club to use to hit your ball to a green. The loft is what enables the ball to come down on the green and stop. This is sometimes referred to as *bite*. A good short iron shot won't run or roll after it hits the green as much as less lofted clubs.

A pitching wedge shot will hold the green after it lands better than will a nine iron shot. It won't roll as much. A nine iron shot won't roll as far as an eight iron.

Your swing remains the same. With experience you come to know just how far the ball will fly in the air for each club and about how far the ball will roll after it lands. That's why you sometimes plan your shots to land in front of the green. You know they will roll onto the green, whereas if you hit the ball to land on the green, it will roll off.

ACCURACY

Your swing is more controlled with any short iron. Accuracy is what you want.

Hollis Stacy pulls a short iron out of her bag as nonchalantly and confidently as the other women pros do. But sometimes she readies herself for the shot a little differently. You might notice a twitch of her nose or hear her humming a bar or two of "The Blue Danube."

Hollis analyzes the swing for a short iron as a little version of the regular swing.

"My stance is slightly open, with feet closer together because the clubs are shorter," she says. "I grip the club with my hands a little ahead of the ball. For most of my shots I do play the ball off my left ear. But for the short irons I move it back toward my nose."

For a short iron shot, Hollis Stacy plays the ball off her nose—off her left heel toward the middle of her stance. Her stance is slightly open, her feet closer together. She grips the club with her hands a little ahead of the ball.

"It's such a pain for me to have to look at my heel when I'm positioning the ball, because I might be aiming another way. That's why I position my ball in line with either my ear or my nose. For these short irons I drop my hands and keep that ball in line with my nose. No problem."

SWING EASILY

Hollis warns, "Don't swing too hard. Don't try to steer short iron shots."

The pros could sing a chorus repeating these cautions about short iron shots: "Swing easy. Swing slow."

When you take a short iron in your hands, Hollis reminds you not to swing too hard. Be conscious of trying to swing easily. Get the feel of swinging easily and in a relaxed manner. Hollis sometimes swings the club back and forth in her left hand only, humming "The Blue Danube" before she puts her right hand on the club.

To be sure of your alignment, put the sole of your club square with the target.

"Take a slow backswing. Keep your left arm straight, but not rigid," Hollis suggests. "Come back a little more upright and not as far as for your other irons. I come down pulling the club with the last three fingers of my left hand so I don't deviate from my swing. I want to follow through toward the pin."

Your short game goes bad when you try to steer the ball. Let the club do the work. Practice trying to make crisp, accurate shots, letting the club go out to the pin.

"My left hand leads from start to finish," Hollis points out. "I take a slow backswing and try to hit the ball with a descending blow without any hurry. I try never to rush the shot. I let both hands go out to the hole."

That is why the short iron shots are more controlled ones. The backswing is not as extended and the follow-through is limited as your need for distance decreases.

Above, left: Slow and easy—that's what Hollis concentrates on for a short iron shot. She takes the club back a little more upright and doesn't sweep it back. She feels only a slight weight shift from left to right. Above, right: Hollis's backswing is shorter with the short irons. Her open stance restricts it.

Above, left: Without hurrying, Hollis lets her left hand lead her downswing. She comes down pulling the club with the last three fingers of her left hand. She wants to hit the ball with a descending blow. She is aware of a slight weight shift back from right to left. Above, right: Hollis concentrates on keeping her left hand firm while coming through the ball. She stays down on it, letting both hands go out toward the hole.

To be sure the ball keeps its momentum, Hollis follows through toward the pin to complete her shot.

"Actually, the shorter clubs and open stance work together to restrict your swing," explains Jerilyn Britz. "You don't have to use your body as much when swinging the short irons."

When she is using her eight iron, Jerilyn thinks of swinging the club from shoulder to shoulder. "Take the club back from the ball in an upright arc to your shoulder. Your right arm will hold the club square with the hole. Aim your downswing at the back of the ball. Let the loft of the club put the ball up. Don't try to scoop it."

SWING FIRMLY

Both the nine iron and the pitching wedge demand more authoritative swings because of the loft of their faces. Keep a firm left hand, break your wrist as you come through the ball, and stay down on the ball, Jerilyn recommends, to keep your swing firm.

You still feel a weight transfer from right to left, but not as much as with the the other irons. Think "down and through the ball." Have the feeling of trying to make crisp, accurate contact of the club with the ball.

You might have the feeling that you are going to stick the club in the ground at the point just under the ball. But you really won't. You'll catch the ball first. The loft of the clubface launches the ball on its way. That's what "down and through the ball" is all about.

There is a special shot you might like to try when you are approaching a green and want the ball to land on it with as little roll as possible.

Shorten your grip on the club, about halfway down. Open the face of the club, noticeably turning the toe of the clubhead to the right. Set your hands way ahead of the club. When you come down to the ball, really whack it with your right hand as you come through.

With practice, there's no reason why you can't hit shots just like Hollis and Jerilyn do. You won't master them right away. But gradually you'll find you are putting the ball up closer to the pin than you were the season before.

SHORTER, MORE UPRIGHT SWING

The swing for the eight and nine irons and the pitching wedge is shorter and more upright than for the other irons. To concentrate on making accurate short iron shots, remember to swing slowly and easily.

You'll succeed if you imitate Hollis.

1. Take a narrow, slightly open stance.
2. Place the ball in line with your nose, back in the center of your stance.

3. Align the sole of the club squarely with the target.

4. Grip the club with your hands a little ahead of the ball.

5. Keep your left arm straight but not rigid. Take the club back in a more upright position, but not as far as your other irons.

6. Feel your weight transfer to the right and back to the left, but do not use your body as much as for other clubs.

7. With the last three fingers of your left hand, pull the club down and through the ball.

8. Follow through, letting both hands go toward the hole.

7
Putting

Stroking the ball on the green into the hole—that's what putting is all about. It's simple and uncomplicated. You take the clubhead of the putter back from the ball, low and straight along the ground. Then bring it back, low and straight along the ground, to stroke the ball solidly.

Fifty percent of the game of golf is supposed to be scored on the putting green. On a par three hole, for example, the player is supposed to be on the green in one stroke, then put her ball into the hole with two more strokes. For a par 5 hole, you're supposed to use three strokes to get on the green, plus two more to get the ball into the hole.

Now, anytime you can use one stroke on the green, instead of the two intended, you're ahead of the game. That's why putting is such an important part of the game of golf.

You can't begin to develop your own putting stroke too soon. A deft putting stroke is the best means a woman has of attaining par scores. Most women can't reach par 4 greens in two. But, if you can get on the green in three shots and hole the putt, you score a par.

That's how you can play as well as a man, though you don't play the game the same way.

Your putting stroke can be as individual as your hairstyle. The pros' putting strokes differ markedly. There are basic fundamentals that are part of any good putting stroke, but just how you apply them depends on what feels comfortable to you.

THE GRIP

Nancy Lopez says she feels her putting in her hands. She uses an interlock putting grip, not common to other players.

Nancy Lopez uses an interlock putting grip. The pinkie of her right hand and the index finger of her left hand lock together. The thumb of her left hand goes under her right hand. Her right index finger is positioned down the grip of the putter.

"With my interlock grip," Nancy explains, "the pinkie of my right hand and the index finger of my left hand lock together. The thumb of my left hand goes under my right hand. I put my right index finger down the grip of the club. This allows me to stroke the club toward the hole a lot better. I am a wrist putter."

This is the under side of Nancy's interlock grip. She believes that the right index finger down the grip of her club allows her to stroke her putter better.

The underside of Jerilyn Britz's reverse overlap grip shows how she places the index finger of her left hand over the pinkie of her right hand.

Jerilyn Britz finds that a reverse overlap grip, a more commonly used putting grip on the tour, works best for her. She places the index finger of her left hand over the little finger of her right hand. She moves her arms and shoulders to move the club. She is a shoulder putter. She does not move her hands or wrists at all when she strokes the ball with her putter.

"I use the same grip as I do on all my clubs," says Hollis Stacy, "the overlap grip." This is the most popular grip among golfers. If you want to brush up on the techniques for the overlap grip, refer to Chapter 2.

Hollis is a combination wrist and shoulder putter. She concentrates on rolling the ball to the hole, following through to the target.

There are players who grip their putters much farther down on the grip than they normally would. You might find that this gives you better control of the stroke.

The cross-hand grip is another grip both pros and amateurs sometimes use. You place the left hand below the right on the grip of the putter. This is not an interlock or an overlap grip. With the left hand below the right, you can keep the left arm and wrist very rigid. Shoulder putters believe this helps keep the wrist firm throughout the putt.

STILL, STILL, STILL

Keep your body and your head still while you putt. That is the first fundamental you must master to be a good putter. Keep your head steady, your eyes directly over the ball.

"I notice that if I allow my hips to move, everything else follows—my head, my eyes. So I concentrate on not moving my hips," reveals Nancy.

"Even the movement of your eyes can have a tendency to move your upper body, which could move the putter blade just a touch—enough to make the ball hit the edge of the hole instead of the middle," warns Jerilyn.

"I don't move before I hit that ball," Hollis states flatly.

Be aware that, if your eyes move to follow the putter blade on your backswing, your head will also move.

Sometimes, when you practice short putts, emphasize keeping your eyes over the ball, with your head steady, by waiting to hear the ball fall into the cup before you move your head. On long putts count "one, two, three" before lifting your head after you strike the ball. Anything you can do to be sure to keep your head still is most important to your putting.

BALL PLACEMENT

Where do you play the ball in your stance to make a good putt? Again, where it feels comfortable to you.

"I play it almost between my two feet, a little closer to my left foot," says Nancy. "My stance is narrow, no wider than my shoulders."

Nancy plays her ball between her feet, closer to her left foot, to putt. Her stance is narrow, her weight evenly on both feet.

"I play the ball very much left for my basic putting stance," notes Jerilyn. "My weight is on my left foot only. The ball is off the toe of my left foot."

"I hit the ball off my left ear," affirms Hollis, keeping to her theory of playing the ball either off her ear or her nose for all of her shots.

Sandra Palmer plays the ball off her left toe, but her right foot is pulled far back from the line. You'll see some of the pros using a squared stance. Others open theirs slightly.

One player keeps her hands on the club even with the ball. Another hold her hands slightly ahead of the ball.

Whenever you have a chance, watch the LPGA's tournaments on TV. Study how the different players putt. You might be able to pick up a point that would improve your own stroke.

Below, left: Jerilyn's ball is very much to the left in her putting stance, off the toe of her left foot. Her weight is on her left foot only.

Below, right: Sandra Palmer plays her ball more from the middle of her putting stance. Her weight is on her left foot. Her right foot is pulled back from her putting line.

THE STROKE

Just how to make a good putting stroke cannot be explained in a one-two-three way.

"I can't explain just how I hit the ball with my putter,"admits Nancy. "I feel it in my hands. I keep the putter low to the ground and slowly take it back. I try to keep my stroke smooth as I come through."

"I allow the putter to swing," says Jerilyn. "I keep it close to the ground on the way back and on the way through. You have to be sure that you have hit the ball, that the ball is well on its way, before you move to look at it," she adds. "There is such a tendency to follow the ball as you strike it."

Below, left: As Jerilyn readies to putt the ball off her left toe, you notice her weight is on her left foot, her right pulled slightly back. She bends over the putt from her waist. Her eyes are over the ball, her arms close to her body, and her legs somewhat flexed. Below, center: Jerilyn brings her putter back low to the ground with her shoulders and arms. Her head remains still. She is a shoulder putter. Below, right: Jerilyn strokes the putter through the ball—follows through. Her head remains over the ball. Her shoulders and arms have moved forward. There is no break in her wrists.

Solid ball contact is what you're after with a putter, as with any of your clubs. The weight of the clubhead naturally accelerates the blade coming through the ball. If you find your putter decelerates through impact, check your backswing. If it is too long, you unconsciously slow your putter coming through the ball because you are afraid of hitting the ball too hard.

"The left hand controls the blade. The right hand is used for power. As you come through, keep the left hand firm to guide the direction of the putter face. If one hand dominates more than the other, it can turn the putter off line a little," Jerilyn points out. "Your hands have to work together."

Some pros flex their right elbow enough to rest it on their right hip bone. That can help keep the club moving in a straight line. If you have a problem with that, you might try imitating that technique.

When you have a really long putt, you do have to grip the club a little harder, a little more firmly. Also, take a longer backswing. But whether the putt is short or long, the same basic rule—"Bring the club back and through low to the ground to stroke the ball solidly"—holds true.

TOUCH

How hard you hit the ball is a matter of feel. A good putter has a good touch. It comes with practice.

Nancy believes you have to have a feel for putting to be a good putter. "I've known some great golfers who can't putt worth a darn," she comments.

Golfers do quote that adage, "There never was a great putter who didn't have a great touch."

If the green is slick, easy does it. If the surface is rough and thick, hit the ball more solidly. If the green is smooth, try lagging your putts. That means that you hit them just enough to slowly roll the ball into the hole. "Died in the hole" is the expression you'll hear players use to describe a lagged putt.

LINING UP

Figuring out where to hit the ball on the green is as important as figuring out how to hit the ball. You'll play with women who always putt for the hole because they can't read the greens; they can't figure out how to direct the ball to the hole other than in a straight line. They are not good putters.

Before you strike the ball, study the green to get a mental picture of where the ball has to go in order to roll into the hole. Walk the green to feel the slope your ball is on. Look at the surface to see which direction the grass is growing in. In golf terminology, that is referred to as the *grain of the green*. If the grain is toward the pin, your ball will roll faster.

Observe the line between your ball and the hole from behind the ball, then from each side. You will also see some pros study the line from behind the hole to the ball. They walk around in a complete circle, observing the ball on the green in relation to the hole. Completely circling the putt is an optional practice. Too much study becomes confusing for many players.

"On a long putt I pick a spot between me and the hole. I line up my ball to that spot," says Nancy. "I'm a spot putter on the long putts but not on the short ones. I just slide the ball up to the hole for those."

"Look from the side. Sometimes you can see a slope better there than from the back or front of the hole," advises Jerilyn. "When you go opposite the ball to read the green, get down to look and see if there is any kind of slope between the hole and the ball."

She sums up her thoughts on lining up, saying, "By the time you get up to the ball and set the blade down, you should have the line set in your mind. Think only of the distance."

Sometimes you'll find that you read a putt one way when you're standing behind it. Then, when you stand up to it, it looks completely different. When that happens to Nancy she negotiates the switch in her mind. Sometimes she changes what she had planned to do. More often, she doesn't. Usually, she finds, your first feeling is the right one.

If you do get confused about the line once you get up to the ball, back away and reline it up. If you simply can't be sure, hit the ball straight. You can't go too far wrong.

SPOT PUTTING

"When I putt I pick out a spot and try to roll the ball over it," states Hollis. "I try to line my whole body up with the line of the putt. I concentrate on placing my body square with the line of the putt. Then I roll the ball."

"When the green has undulations," Nancy suggests, "try to figure out the spot where the ball is going to break from the line where you hit it to roll into the cup. Then hit the ball toward that spot. Just stroke the ball there," she cautions.

"Breaking putts are challenging. You can't roll the ball directly to the cup on a green with mounds and angles. You roll it along a line you think will break into the hole. To putt, you don't look at the hole. You look at the line where you want your ball to go."

When you're faced with a big break, Jerilyn suggests that you pick a spot just a few inches directly in front of the ball to aim for. Hit the putt as if it's straight to that spot.

"If you try to putt the ball on the breaking line, you will probably pull it or push it, trying to help it follow the line," she warns. "Whereas, once you've picked a spot to aim for, you can concentrate on how hard to hit the ball." Those spots the pros refer to are marks on the green that they see—perhaps a blade of grass, a different color in the green, anything that differs in appearance from the rest of the green that you can use as a spot. How far the spot should be from your ball depends on you. Some spot putters use one about a foot from their ball to keep their follow-through on line. Most determine the spot in relation to the distance of the putt.

Speed-break putts are the most challenging putts to sink. They are typically sidehill and downhill lies. The success of the putt depends not only on how well you read the break of the green, but also on how hard you hit the ball to play the break.

Elation describes the feeling of sinking one.

DIFFERENCES

Downhill putts, uphill ones, putts off the green, putting out of sand traps—such putts can boggle the mind of an amateur. But the pros have practical approaches to all of them.

"If you have quick greens and you are hitting the putt downhill, if you put the ball off the toe of your putter, the outer edge, you can stroke it normally," explains Nancy. "The ball will roll slower. If you line the putt up on the toe of your putter, the ball comes off much softer. It does work," she assures.

On really fast downhill putts, you can end up three putting very easily. So concentrate on making a good effort the first time. Concentrate on distance.

Pick a spot before the hole to aim for. Then look at that spot before the hole when you're aiming your ball. If the green is really fast, pick a spot halfway between you and the hole. Try to hit only that far. The ball will continue to roll.

If you're coming uphill, look at a spot that is behind or beyond the hole. This way you are more likely to hit the ball hard enough to get up to the hole.

Many pros pull out a putter to use when their ball is off the green. It gives them a better feel of distance when they can roll the ball on the ground.

If you have longer grass to go through, but not much, close or hood the clubhead (turn the top of the blade over, slightly forward). Hit the ball off the ground from the middle of your stance.

You can use a putter out of a bunker if the pin is very close and the sand is rather compact and even with the edge of the grass. Again, hood your putter blade a little. Be sure you hit the ball before you hit the sand to put overspin on the ball. If

To use a putter from long grass at the edge of the green, Jerilyn first hoods the face of her putter, opens her stance, then hits the ball from back in the middle of her stance. From her follow-through, you can judge that she hit the ball harder than normally.

you have to go up over the lip of a trap, do not use a putter. There is too great a chance that the lip will catch the ball and bounce it back into the trap or the ball will wedge into the lip.

PRESSURE

Nowhere can pressure loom up in front of your ball as it does on the putting green. When women start betting beyond nickel and dime stakes, little three-foot putts can become unbearably difficult. "The game's not fun anymore," Nancy says, "when the betting gets out of hand."

However, to play competitive golf of any kind you do have to learn to handle the pressure of the sport. So often this is manifested on the putting green when a match or tournament is won by a single putt.

Prepare for pressure putts before you encounter them.

Nancy believes this can help. "Go to the practice putting green and practice those putts that are really the important ones, the five- and six-footers. Those are the ones that you are expected to make and that you expect yourself to make. When you don't, your confidence fades—and with it your concentration. Practice them so much that when you are on the golf course you just think of the basics.

"Whenever I have a five-footer, with a lot of pressure on it, I just kind of put myself back on the putting green. I stand over the ball and concentrate on keeping the putter low and slow, back and through, keeping my stroke smooth. I concentrate

Below, left: When Nancy practices those five- to six-footers, she concentrates on the basics. Her ball is slightly forward of center. Her feet are parallel to each other and the line of the putt. She bends over the putt from the waist, so her eyes are over the ball. Her arms are held out a little from her body. Her legs are straight. Below, center: Nancy brings her club back low, though not as close to the ground as Jerilyn does. Notice that Nancy's arms remain in position. Her wrists break to take the putter back. Below, right: At impact, Nancy's putter is square with the ball, her eyes over it. Her wrists direct her hands. She is a wrist putter.

Above, left: Nancy's putter follows through the stroke. Her shoulders remain in position. Her wrists bring her hands forward. Above, right: As the ball moves forward, there is no relaxation in Nancy's stance. Her body and head remain still.

totally on what I have to do in order to erase the pressure I might feel.''

She adds, "When you step over the putt and feel yourself tightening up because you want to make that putt so badly, take a big deep breath. Relieve it audibly. I do this and it relaxes my shoulders, everything.''

You'll notice that, to get relaxed, different pros go through different routines when they set up to putt. Some step back a little from the line of the putt. Keeping their feet together, they take a couple of practice putts to loosen up. As others stand over the ball they mentally direct themselves to relax. Observe what works for them. It could help you.

As the ball is about to go into the cup, Nancy has unconsciously brought her putter back to position. There is a slight change in her head, but her body has remained still throughout the sequence.

PRACTICE

Sooner or later the best of putters go cold. Don't let it get you down. Go out and practice. You've probably unconsciously changed some little thing. You're picking the putter up, jerking it, or maybe forgetting to come through.

Your putting game can be strong whether you hit a drive 50 yards or 150 yards. It's up to you to develop the feel, the touch with the blade that puts your ball in the hole more often than not.

How hard you hit the ball with a putter is a matter of feel that comes with practice. And nowhere is the feeling "I can do it" more important to success than on the putting green.

When you practice you don't always have to use a putting green. Some women have found that the indoor-outdoor carpeting in their kitchen or on their patio makes a good putting surface. Look around your house or apartment. Figure out where you can work on your putting stroke for a few minutes every so often. You'll be pleasantly surprised at how well your stroke develops with that kind of practice.

Putting is one part of the game in which every woman can excel. But you do have to work at it.

Apply the basics of good putting to develop a consistently good stroke of your own.

1. Grip your club with equal pressure in both hands, using an overlap, reverse overlap, interlocking, or cross-hand grip.

2. Place the ball in your stance where it feels comfortable, with your eyes directly over the ball.

3. Keep your body and your head still as you stroke the putter.

4. Stroke the putter, straight and low to the ground, back from and through the ball.

5. Stroke the putter slowly and smoothly to strike the ball solidly.

6. How hard you stroke the ball is a matter of feel.

7. Learn to read greens.

8. Practice to gain confidence.

8

The Driver

Work up to your driver. It's the hardest club in your bag to learn to use well. Before you try to play with your driver off the tee, enjoy success using your five wood, your four wood, and your three wood.

Work everything from the easiest club to the most difficult. The driver is your most difficult club to hit. You can hit a three wood off the tee almost as far and you'll hit it more easily. Don't try to use the driver until you are playing golf fairly well.

"A lot of women get into trouble right away with the driver because they try to hit it too hard," comments Beth Daniel. "Golf is not a power game for a woman. It's a game of accuracy. Concentrate on accuracy. It is also important to stay smooth. Use your normal swing with the driver. Let the club do the work."

At first you might not get much distance when you do start to play with your driver. It is harder to swing because it is the

115

longest club you have. But if you've been using your three and four woods regularly, you won't be afraid to swing it. Distance will come in time. Don't change your swing. Just keep swinging it as you do your three and four woods.

Beth and Judy Rankin are excellent players off the tee. They apply the same basic fundamentals.

FOCUS

Beth focuses on a sweeping action when she is setting up for her drive. She wants to sweep her club back from the ball and then through, to give herself square, accurate contact with the ball at top clubhead speed.

Judy Rankin focuses on swinging her driver through the ball toward the target. "Swing the club. Really let the club go," she emphasizes.

Whether you focus on a sweeping or swinging motion when you are setting up for your drive, it is most important to focus your concentration in order to hit your drive well.

THE ADDRESS

Judy Rankin plays the ball a little farther forward in her stance when she takes her driver in hand. "My stance is shoulder wide, fairly square. At address I bend my legs slightly. My hands grip the club in a straight line from my shoulder. You have to get your weight to your right side as you make your backswing. As I lift my club, I roll my left foot inward to shift my weight. My arms and shoulders pivot as I take the club back."

Beth's stance is also shoulder wide. "If you get any wider or narrower than shoulder width, you are going to run into problems," she warns.

How far you stand from the ball depends on how long your upper body is and how long your arms are. Basically, whatever distance feels right for you and allows you room to make a full shoulder turn when you bring back the club is correct.

Beth Daniel uses a 10-finger grip to hold her driver. Her ball is played inside her left heel, with her left foot very slightly open, teed up for her driver. She puts her feet shoulder width apart and flexes her legs. Notice that her hands are just slightly ahead of the ball.

Beth keeps her left arm straight as she sweeps her club back with her shoulders leading. Her weight shifts from her left to her right side as her body turns.

At the top of her backswing, Beth's shoulder is under her chin. Her firm right leg and left leg bent inward indicate her weight shift to her right foot. She pauses to set her hands.

As Beth shifts her weight back forward to her left foot, her body moves out of the way. There is room for her arms to come down, bringing her clubhead with them.

Beth drives everything through to her left. Her weight is back on her left foot, her hips rotate to the left, and her left shoulder leads her left arm, pulling the club down.

Sweeping through her swing toward the target, Beth's club achieves square, accurate contact with the ball at top club-head speed.

Beth positions her ball off the inside of her left heel. "I know it used to be taught to start with the driver inside the left heel and then move the ball back as you go into the irons. But I play the ball off the inside of my left heel, no matter what wood or iron I'm using."

When she addresses the ball Beth sets her hands ahead of the clubhead at the crease in the left leg of her slacks. "That puts them just a hair ahead of the ball, which is where they should be," she observes. "They shouldn't be behind the ball or too far in front of it."

To line up, put your clubface square with the ball as Beth does. It is also square with the line of target. Be sure your body is parallel to that target line, even if your left foot is slightly open, as Beth's is.

Stand slightly bent at the waist with a slight flex in your knees. Feel your weight on the balls of your feet.

YOUR SWING

"Bring your club back with your shoulders," directs Beth. "As you begin your backswing, keep your head still. Sweep your club along the ground about 18 inches as you gradually turn your upper body and shoulders to bring your arms up to the top of your backswing.

"Keep your left arm straight but not rigid. It should never be so rigid as to restrict your shoulder turn. As your shoulders turn, shift your weight to your right side. At the top of your backswing, your left shoulder should be under your chin."

Pause slightly at the top of your backswing. That pause enables your hands to set. Your weight shifts back to the left foot. Then your body can move out of the way, your arms following as you come down with the club.

"I drive everything to my left side through to the target on my downswing," explains Beth. "My arms are going to the target. My head comes up naturally to allow me to follow through."

On occasion, you will notice a player with a short, rigid

As Beth swings her arms toward the target, her head comes up naturally, allowing her to follow through.

Beth finishes high. She completes her follow-through looking at the hole.

backswing who hits the ball well. Such a swing is effective for her because the individual has developed unique wrist action and strength in the upper body. But it is not the type of swing best suited for most women to imitate.

FOLLOW-THROUGH

Distance comes from extending through the ball—finishing with your hands high.

Beth believes that many women don't achieve the follow-through they could. She thinks it's because they are too concerned about keeping their heads down. "When your head is down your arms can only go so far," she declares. "If you just let your arms go to the target, your head is going to come up naturally. That allows you to follow through. Don't worry so much about keeping your head down. It restricts your follow-through if you do."

Beth emphasizes: Sweep the club through the ball toward the target. Finish by looking at the hole to get the accuracy and distance you want from your driver. Finish with your club up and over your left shoulder to give your ball a chance to fly long and straight.

"Swing at your target at all times. The minute you quit on a shot, you lose a tremendous amount of distance. You cut it off."

To be effective with your driver, grip the club firmly. As you shift your weight, sweep it back slowly to the top of your backswing. Come down and forward, sweeping your club through the ball, extending through to the target. Finish high.

"Work on your follow-through," admonishes Judy. "Too many women take the club back beautifully. Then they tend to hit at the ball rather than through it. If you hit at the ball, you will hit it. But there's nothing beyond that. Your club will turn. The ball will go left or right. You have no momentum going. You lose distance."

This curve in Beth Daniel's body line reflects the timing in her swing that enables her to bring her clubhead through the flat area of her swing behind the ball at top clubhead speed. The lower part of her body appears to be ahead of her upper body. This acceleration of clubhead speed at impact in all the pros' swings is what gives them the distance and accuracy they achieve.

HIT THE BALL

To hit the ball solidly, come through the hitting area, swinging freely, extending toward the target. Let your clubhead give the ball a good whack. As Hollis Stacy says, "Hit it hard."

When you want to increase the distance your driver obtains after you've been hitting it well for quite a while, work on rhythm and timing to obtain the greatest amount of natural clubhead release at impact. This means that you should learn the timing necessary to be behind the ball at impact.

The curve that you see in the pros' body lines when they are coming through the ball manifests this timing, this ability to stay behind the ball at impact.

Judy Rankin explains it in simple terms. "Staying behind the ball means that the upper half of your body stays behind the ball. You shift to your right, swinging back from the ball. Swinging to the ball, the lower part of your body shifts back to your left side first. If you can keep the upper part of your body from going back at the same moment the lower part is moving, you are then behind the ball."

Actually achieving this movement in your swing is not easy. Work with a pro to develop it. If you can master the timing, you'll be amazed at the increased yardages in your drives. But it's not something to work on initially in your game.

KEYS

While you're learning, and long afterward, key thoughts can be important aids to your swing.

"I have different ones, depending on what I'm trying to work on in my swing at the time," says Beth. "Right now my keys are *slow* and *firm*. *Slow* on the backswing and keep my hands *firm* when I am coming down. It's important to have keys, but not too many. Two are plenty. If you get any more than that, then you're thinking of too much."

HOOK AND SLICE

Once you've got your drive down and send one after another straight and far down the fairway, your game off the tee is well in hand. Then again, challenges do arise. Here and there is a hole where, if you hit your drive straight and far down the middle, trouble waits.

Some fairways turn to the right or to the left, maybe 135 yards from the tee. If you want to use your driver off those tees, you have to direct your ball to the right or to the left.

When you want to hit your ball radically to the right, you use what is referred to as a *slice*. A ball that curves more gradually to the right is referred to as a *fade*. A ball hit radically to the left is called a *hook*. A more gradual change in direction to the left is termed a *draw*.

Beth believes that the easiest way to effect either a slice or a hook is to grip your club with the face either open or closed.

To open the clubface, position the toe of the club to the right as you address the ball. To close the clubface, position the toe of the club to the left as you address the ball.

To fade a drive off the tee, Beth says, "Open the face of your driver, then grip the club. Address the ball with an open stance—your left foot drawn back from the line of flight. Take your normal swing. When you come to impact the clubface is going to be open. The ball will slice, going to the right as it flies.

"To draw a tee shot, close the face of your driver. Then grip the club. Close your stance—your right foot drawn back from the line of flight. Take your normal swing. When you come to impact the clubface is going to be closed. The ball will draw."

If you grip the driver, then open its face, the ball won't slice. The clubface will not be open at impact. If you grip the driver, then close its face, you won't hook the ball.

Whether you want to slice or hook your drive, the most important point to remember is: Open or close the face of the club first; then grip the club.

As you practice, you'll learn how far to open or close your stance to get the degree of slice or hook you want. You can become as adept as the pros at driving your ball left or right off the tee.

BASICS

Hit a drive straight and far down the fairway. You can do it time and time again when you follow this procedure:

1. Grip the club correctly and firmly.
2. Keep your stance shoulder wide with your weight balanced evenly on the balls of your feet.

3. Position your ball off your left heel, or slightly forward of that, if you prefer.

4. Bend your body at the waist and flex your legs.

5. Place your arms comfortably away from your body with your hands just slightly ahead of the clubhead.

6. Line up the clubhead square with the ball and the target. Be sure your body is parallel to the target line.

7. Sweep the driver back slowly, straight, and low from the ball. Turn your shoulders and upper body gradually, shifting your weight to your right. Bring your arms to the top of your backswing, keeping your left arm straight.

8. Pause slightly at the top of your backswing to set your wrists and initiate your weight shift back to your left side.

9. Come down, moving your lower body out of the way, to allow your arms to follow through, swinging your club freely through impact, extending toward the target.

10. Complete your follow-through, bringing the club up and over your left shoulder. Finish looking at the hole.

9
The Long Irons

Hitting a long iron shot solidly, straight, and far is a thrill. It is one of the toughest shots for a woman to make in golf.

Before you can hit a two, three, or four iron well, you do have to develop a good basic swing. Only the woman who hits a club strongly should use a long iron regularly. The long iron game is the one part of a woman's game in which strength is a factor.

Dot Germaine frequently uses her long irons. Whenever she needs a long, low, accurate shot in tournament play she pulls out a three or four iron. You can observe Judy Rankin and Jan Stephenson using a two iron regularly. But generally, women, even other pros, are not enthusiastic about using long irons. They are difficult clubs for women to hit well.

THE CHALLENGE

What is it that makes hitting a good long iron shot such a

Dot Germain shows the difference in the lengths of the five and three irons in her set. That longer length of the three iron is one of the reasons amateurs find it hard to hit.

challenge? The club itself. The longer length of the club shaft combined with its straight clubface intimidates the average woman golfer. You probably wonder how you can get the ball up in the air using a club like that. So you try to help the ball. Try to scoop it or hit at it as hard as you can. But neither approach works.

THE SWING

"Most players think you have to swing differently when you take a long iron in hand," Dot explains. "But that isn't the case. The loft of the clubface is the reason the club is harder to use to get the ball up. But you don't need a different swing to manage it. Your swing should be the same as it is for your other irons. If you are hitting your seven iron well, you can use the same swing to hit your long iron well.

"However, it is most important to make a full swing when you use a long iron," she emphasizes.

Because the club is longer, the timing of your swing is also particularly important. You have to give yourself time to make a full backswing. The long shaft demands that you give yourself the time necessary to complete your backswing. Slow down. Don't hurry the shot. Solid contact is what you are after when the face of the club meets the ball. Make *smooth, even tempo* your key thought.

"Grip your club as you always do," advises Dot. "But you can position the ball a little farther forward in your stance, if that feels more comfortable for you. Keep your stance shoulder wide."

Dot holds her three iron with an overlap grip. She keeps her stance shoulder wide and plays the ball a little farther forward in her stance for long iron shots.

She suggests that you might try to keep a little more weight on your right at address to keep your upper body behind the ball as you come through on the shot.

As you take your club back, sweep the clubface back, brushing it lightly over the grass. That enhances your tempo and helps you to make a complete backswing. Good weight shift from your left foot to your right, then back to your left as you swing, allows you to contact the ball solidly as you come through.

Below, left: Dot sweeps her long iron back slowly, brushing lightly over the grass, as she shifts her weight from left to right. Below, right: It is important to complete the backswing with a long shafted three iron, so there is plenty of room for a good downswing. Notice how Dot's club is almost parallel to the ground.

Above, left: With a well-timed forward thrust, Dot brings her iron down, shifting her weight back to her left. She keeps her left arm straight, extending it toward the hole to be certain she keeps a full swing arc. Above, right: Dot stays down on the ball to use her clubhead speed coming through the ball. Any divot she takes comes after she hits the ball, not before.

"Keep your left arm straight. Hit the ball first," Dot says. "Stay down on the ball to use your clubhead speed as you come through it. Any divot you take must come after you hit the ball, not before."

With a well-timed forward swing, your weight will gradually shift back to your left foot. Your upper body will stay behind the ball.

"Don't worry whether the ball goes left or right. As long as it is going forward well, you have a good long iron shot," comments Dot. "Amateurs tend to be too hard on themselves, expect too much from their shots."

A complete follow-through gives Dot's long iron shots the distance and accuracy she expects from them.

Follow through. Follow-through is the key to a successful long iron shot just as it is for any other golf shot. If you keep in mind *follow-through*, you're not so liable to spoil your shot trying to scoop or hit down on the ball.

Once you do start to hit the long irons you can get spin on them. The more backspin and the higher you want the ball, the more you must stay down with the ball. That almost seems a contradiction. To get the ball up, you stay down. It takes practice. But the rewards are accurately placed, soul-satisfying long iron shots like those that Dot and the other pros make.

HITTING DOWN

Scooping, trying to help your ball up with your club, is the most common error golfers make with their irons. You end up topping the ball. It goes nowhere.

There are pros and instructors who emphasize hitting down on long irons to get the ball airborne. That is tough. Too often amateur golfers, in a mistaken attempt to hit down on the ball, hack at it instead. That's why Dot suggests, "Meet the ball solidly and follow through rather than trying to hit down on the ball."

But if you feel strong enough, if the challenge of learning to hit down on the ball appeals to you, work on it with a pro. To hit down on a ball, you have to learn to move off your right side quickly. Hit down on the ball as if you want to take a divot right under it. Actually, you do hit down on the ball and keep your club on it as long as you can to develop a divot. But you take that divot after you hit the ball. As you come through your shot, you are coming through the ground behind the ball to take the divot.

Trying to accomplish this swing on your own could ruin your own basic swing. So, if you want to try it, do it with caution. Work it out with a professional instructor's help.

YOUR FOUR IRON

There's no question. You need a four iron in your bag. There are times when you are going to have to use an iron that doesn't get as much loft as the other clubs in your bag. Learn to use your four iron for those shots. Work with it and learn to use it well. When your swing is developed you can count on 120 yards or more from your four iron. You'll pull it out whenever you need a long, straight accurate shot.

When you try to get a lot of distance with your three or four irons or try to do too much with the clubs, you can complicate your swing. You end up slowing down as you come through the ball, not making solid contact with it. Then you miss the shot.

It's a fact: The natural flexibility a woman has in her body is a decided asset for making good long iron shots. Keep your shoulders turning as you swing to create a full swing arc. It's the coordinated movements of your legs, hips, shoulders, arms, and hands that result in clubhead speed coming through the ball. Good clubhead speed at impact guarantees solid ball contact every time. And that's what you want when you pull a long iron out of your bag.

With a couple of key swing thoughts in mind, keep your swing simple. Then your long irons will be effective when you need to use them.

PRACTICE SWINGS

If you take a practice swing, make it count to help you get tempo for your real shot. Swing at something—a tuft of grass, a leaf—as though you were actually hitting the ball. The feel of that smooth practice swing should transfer to your real shot.

"The problem with women and long irons is practice," says Dot. "They are longer clubs with less loft. You can't use them well if you don't practice hitting with them."

WHEN TO USE

Just when do you pull a two or three iron out of your bag? Only if you are a very strong player is it worth keeping a two iron. Some women pros do use a two iron quite regularly, but not many. On reflection, they don't believe that what an amateur can get from the club is worth the time you would have to spend learning to hit it.

Whether you use a three iron or not depends on your swing. A good three iron shot can get 130 or more yards for many women. But today, many manufacturers are replacing the three iron in their standard sets and adding a seven wood in place of it. They say too many women have problems hitting a three iron.

If you want a three iron in your set, you can get one. Many amateurs, as well as pros, carry both a three iron and a seven wood. The three iron is more accurate than a wood. When you hit it well, it flies straight and true.

Even though you hit a seven wood about the same distance as a three iron, you will want to use the iron if the shot has to stay low or is going into the wind. Sometimes you can use a long iron from the rough if the grass is not above the middle of the ball and the ball needs to stay low. But be very selective about using that shot.

When a good golfer needs strategy shots, you'll see her select a three or four iron to make them. For instance, off the tee of a par three hole or off the tee of a tight hole, you can hit a more accurate shot with a long iron. Tee the ball high and sweep it as you would a driver. Remember, let the clubhead do the work.

Never try for the miraculous shot, like sending a perfect three or four iron shot low under hanging branches through trees to a green. Admit that the shot is not in your repertoire. Get out of trouble first. You have more chance for those miracle shots around the green.

When you do have to hit an iron over some trees or get it up in the air more than you normally would for some other reason, you do have to change your address. Play the ball as much forward as you can in your stance to catch it on the upswing. Don't take your club back as far as you ordinarily do. Break your hands quicker to hit the ball as you come through on your upswing to get it up. Whatever distance you are from your target, take one more club than you otherwise would. You are going to lose distance to height. If you ordinarily hit your four iron 120 yards, and the shot you are looking at is 120 yards but has to be high to miss a clump of small trees, then use your three iron to be certain of clearing those trees and still making the 120 yards.

EXERCISES

If you are interested, here are a couple of exercises you can do to help develop the wrist and forearm strength you need to be a strong iron player.

1. Twist a towel in your hands. As you wring, the left hand moves away from your body and the right hand moves toward your body.

2. Keep a rubber ball handy in your car or beside the TV to squeeze in your hands when you have the time.

BASIC LONG IRON SWING

When you take a long iron in hand to make a shot you need, you can make a good one if you remember these tips:

1. Take your usual shoulder-wide stance.
2. Position the ball slightly farther forward (to the left) than you ordinarily do.
3. Grip the club as usual, with the last three fingers of your left hand firmly around the club.
4. Bring the club back slowly on the backswing, sweeping the clubface lightly over the grass as your weight shifts to your right foot.
5. Be certain to complete your backswing.
6. As your weight shifts back to your left foot for the downswing, keep your upper body behind the ball.
7. Keeping a straight left arm, hit the ball solidly as you come through.
8. Follow through completely to finish the shot.
9. Make *smooth, even tempo* your key thought.

10
Special Shots

"Hitting the ball solidly is the key to playing golf well. And so often that's what a woman doesn't do when she has to hit a special shot," observes Judy Rankin.

Faced with a ball on a downhill or uphill lie or in any other unusual position, your ordinary swing often disappears. You replace it with a kind of body lunge augmented with an arms-and-hands swing to muscle the ball into the air. The ball goes nowhere.

"Anxiety is probably one good reason for this," Judy offers. "You just can't wait to hit that ball. Get the shot over with."

No matter where the ball lies, the rhythm in your swing, combined with determination to let the clubhead do its work, is the key to making a good special shot.

"Don't worry about changing your swing for different lies," Judy counsels. "When you change the ball position that is enough for most needs."

YOUR SWING

For most of the special shots you have to play on the course during a round, swing as you always do. Changing the ball position or opening or closing your stance to make a special shot shouldn't change the pattern of your swing.

Take a good grip on the club. Judy does favor a strong grip for women. She describes it as "turning your left hand more toward your right side on the club." She uses the grip for all of her shots. It gives her a stronger swing and helps keep her ball on line, she believes.

Whether you use a grip like Judy's or an ordinary overlap grip, be certain to grasp the club firmly to make a special shot.

SETTING UP

"Take your time setting up for unfamiliar shots," advises Judy. "There is a certain way to set up to the ball that is better than other ways. It is especially important when you are confronted with an unusual shot.

"Line up the golf club first. Put the clubhead where you want to aim the ball. Then position your left foot. That is the foot you want to position the golf ball to. Then, let your right foot move into place. Never set your right foot down first."

When Judy Rankin sets up for a shot, she lines up the golf club first, putting the clubhead where she wants to aim the ball. Then she positions her feet—left foot first, then the right.

Judy plays the ball off her left foot for almost every shot. With an iron her stance is narrower than for a wood. That brings her ball position closer to the center of her stance.

Play the ball off your left heel for almost every club in your bag. With the irons, as your clubs get shorter, your stance will get narrower. That brings your left heel closer to the center of your body. But no matter what club you use, the more often you hit the ball off the same spot, the more often you're going to hit the ball the same way.

The only time you move the ball in your stance is to play special shots.

WEIGHT SHIFT

"The most important part of any good swing," Judy points out, "is good weight shift to your right side, then back to your left side. This is true no matter where you ordinarily make the swing."

As you take the club back, shift your weight to your right side. At the top of your backswing, pause. Set your hands. Let your lower body initiate the shift back to your left side to make the downswing. That keeps your upper body behind the ball as you swing the club through to the target.

"When you are really letting the club go, you will strike the back side of the golf ball at top acceleration," states Judy. "If

Above, left: As Judy takes her club back, her weight shifts to her right side. But note how steady her head remains as her hips and shoulders turn, her straight left arm bringing the club back. Above, right: In this photo of the top of Judy's backswing, you see that her weight has completely shifted to her firm right leg. Her straight left arm helps give her a full, wide arc on her downswing.

you try to direct the club to the ball at impact, the club slows down so much that you miss the shot. You cut off the natural release of the clubhead. You can't follow through.''

Hitting the ball solidly as you come through, swinging freely, is part of the proper synchronization of movement that you develop in your swing. Actually, you don't think about it; it just happens when you swing with rhythm and tempo.

So often the part of your swing that goes when you have to make a speical shot is rhythm and tempo. It's most common. To get the shot over with, you rush it.

You have to learn to play a ball correctly off a slope or a hill to score well. With direction, you can handle these special

Only a camera could stop Judy's swing at this point. It gives you a chance to see the synchronization of movement between her body and her club as she swings freely through the ball. It is a great example of the rhythm and timing in the pros' swings that amateurs want to imitate.

shots easily. With practice, you'll become confident in hitting them.

Imitate Judy's approach when you find your ball resting on an uphill slope or below you on the side of a hill. Take your time. Concentrate on what you have to do to make your shot. Then make it effectively.

BALL POSITION

To play most specialized shots, you have to change the position of the ball in your address. It's necessary in order to hit the ball first. Take a practice swing or two to see where the bottom of your swing is—where the club first contacts the ground. Then put your ball just to the right of that spot.

Sometimes, in order to play some of the specialized shots, you also have to change your body position at address. That depends on the shot.

UPHILL

"When you're standing on the side of a hill, where your left foot is higher than your right, move the ball forward in your

When you are on the side of a hill where your left foot is higher than your right, move the ball forward in your stance as Judy does. Aim the ball a bit right.

stance," says Judy. "Take a couple of practice swings to determine just where the bottom of your swing is and to get a feel for the shot."

There is a tendency to pull the ball (hit it to the left) with this type of lie. Compensate by aiming the ball a bit to the right.

If the uphill lie is very steep, flex your left knee more as you address the ball. Switch to a less lofted club to get more distance with your shot.

DOWNHILL

On a downhill lie, where your right foot is higher than

On a downhill lie, where your right foot is higher than your left, play the ball back in your stance as Judy does. Even though this hill is not steep, Judy chokes down a little on her club, so the hill doesn't get in the way of her swing. She aims the ball a bit left.

your left, Judy says, "Move the ball back in your stance if the hill gets in your way." The ball has a tendency to slice (go to the right) from this address. So try to aim more to the left.

If the hill is quite steep, flex your right knee more to help keep your balance. The down slope of the hill will hood the blade of your club more, so use a more lofted club.

To play uphill and downhill special shots, remember:

1. Play the ball off the foot that is higher on the hill.
2. Flex the knee more that is higher on the hill.
3. Take a couple of practice swings to see where the bottom of the swing is and to get a feel for the swing.

BALL ABOVE YOU

When you find yourself standing below your ball—that is, the ball is above you on the side of a hill—choke down on your club to grip it. Grasp it toward the bottom of the handle. Holding the club shorter keeps you from hitting the hill first.

When you take your stance, stand more erect than you usually do. But flex your knees so your weight isn't back on your heels. Otherwise, you can lose your balance when you swing. Play the ball just slightly back in your stance. Concentrate on keeping your head steady.

Aim the ball a little to the right, as it's inclined to go left from this spot. If the slope is severe, cut down on your body turn to keep your balance.

When Judy finds herself standing below the ball, she plays it slightly back in her stance and chokes down on her club. She stands more erect but flexes her knees so her weight isn't all back on her heels.

BALL BELOW YOU

"If the ball is below you, stand closer for your swing. The key to a good shot is to get close enough to the ball so you don't lose your balance when you swing," reveals Judy Rankin. "Be close enough to keep your weight solid on your feet, on your heels, so you don't fall over on your toes. You don't have to change the position of the ball much. Perhaps play it back toward the middle of your stance a little. But do move closer to the ball than you ordinarily stand."

Try to bend more from your waist to address a ball that is downhill from you so you don't fall over it when you swing your club. You can't shift your weight normally in this position as you swing, so there is a minimal body movement. Do keep your arms and hands firm as you're coming through the ball. This is a difficult shot. Control your swing and don't swing hard to play it.

When you find yourself standing above your ball, be certain to stand close enough for your swing, as Judy is. If the hill were steeper, Judy would bend over even more from her waist to be certain to catch the ball and not lose her balance.

Aim accordingly. From this position the ball flies farther right than normally.

As you practice and play these shots, you'll become more familiar with how to hit them and with the direction the ball takes when you do.

OVER THE TREES

When you need to hit the ball over some trees or especially high, move it forward in your stance. You do that to try to catch the ball on your upswing. To do the job, be sure you pull the most lofted wood or iron from your bag. And don't forget that you need one club more to make up the distance you lose to loft. That is, if you normally need a five wood to hit 130 yards, take a four wood to loft a 130-yard shot.

Take your stance with your feet, shoulders, and hips aligned to the left of the target but with the clubface aimed to the right. Place your hands about even with the ball. Such a stance limits your backswing. But be certain to sweep through the ball and finish high, looking at the target, to make the most effective shot.

You'll need a lot of practice to learn how to do this one. But, if you aim to be a low-handicap player, practice, practice, practice.

UNDER THE TREES

When you need to keep your shot low, play the ball back in your stance. Put your hands ahead of the ball and tilt the clubface forward slightly. Aim the bottom of the clubface at the target. Keep your left arm straight. With your weight primarily on your left side, take the clubhead back low. Again, you won't be able to take an ordinary backswing with this stance. But be certain to swing the clubhead out toward the target to complete the shot.

OVER WATER

Water, even the smallest pond, can loom as large as an ocean when you have to hit a golf ball over it. You can blow a good round putting at least one ball into water that you could hit over without any problem if it were fairway yardage twice as long.

There is something about water that shoots a player's confidence to specks, demolishing the best of swings. But you have to overcome this to score well. Conquer the demon.

"Think where the ball *should* go," advocates Judy, "not where it *could* go. It's undeniably true that the more uncertain you are, the faster you swing. And a speedy backswing will ruin your entire swing every time. Think rhythm and tempo. Don't ever rush your shot. Key yourself with words like *smooth, slow*. Count to yourself. It can help."

TROUBLE

Anytime you get into trouble on the course, the first thing to do is get out. Lots of times you'll be tempted to go for it, give an impossible shot a try, especially when your game is going well. Don't.

Playing it safe is very difficult for most amateurs to do, the pros observe. They can't believe the shots that they see amateurs try to make during a Pro-Am round. The pros would never attempt many shots that amateurs show no hesitation to try.

Get out of trouble first. Take the penalty, if necessary. Playing the percentages pays off. Too often, one bad shot just leads to another and another and another.

When you find your ball in a position that calls for a special shot, you can play it well and confidently if you recall some fundamentals.

1. Take your time to consider what you have to do to hit the ball well under the circumstances.

2. Take a couple of practice swings to determine where the

bottom of your swing is and to get a feel for it.

3. Position the ball in your stance as necessary to play the shot.

4. Position your body and clubface as necessary to play the shot.

5. Before you swing, say to yourself, *rhythm* and *tempo*. Swing smoothly.

11

Bunker Shots

"Have fun with your bunker play. Don't be afraid of the sand," cajoles Hollis Stacy. "Bunkers are a woman's number one handicap. Land in one and you're petrified. You try to scoop the ball out or dig it out. And you know that's not going to work."

"Now, if you're just a beginner, don't try to play out of a bunker when you get into one your first few times on the course," advises Sandra Palmer. "Take your ball out of the sand and chip it up. A sand shot is different from all the others in golf. Wait until you have some experience playing before you attempt one."

You can approach a sand shot with know-how and confidence when you have an understanding of what it is all about.

THE CLUB

You have to use a special club to get your ball out of a bunker. It's called a *sand wedge*, a *utility wedge*, or whatever a

149

manufacturer chooses. It is built differently from other clubs. Its back edge is higher, its sole wider, its face bigger. You also use it differently than you do other clubs.

"You have to use the right kind of club to get out of the sand," insists Hollis. "Not a real heavy club, but one with a flange on the bottom of it that will bounce the ball out of the sand—enable the sand to bounce the ball out. To make that flange work for you, cock your hands a little bit and swing your arms. There's a natural wrist break. But it's more of an arm motion swing. Come down hitting the sand behind the ball. Then the bounce of the club takes the ball.

Hollis Stacy makes the flange of her sand wedge work for her. She hits the sand behind the ball and the bounce takes the ball out of the sand.

"The most important part of a sand shot is to utilize that bounce that comes from using the flange of the club," says Hollis emphatically. "You can't be afraid to take sand if you're going to do it."

Sandra Palmer agrees. "You have to use a sand wedge to be able to get out of the sand. The bottom of the club is designed to do that."

Don't be afraid to take sand to get out of a bunker. Sandra Palmer shows that the bottom of a sand wedge was designed to get the ball up and out of it when you do.

A DIFFERENT SHOT

"The sand shot is the only shot in golf where you do not hit the ball first," Sandra declares. "For any other shot in the game you want to hit the ball first. But for a sand shot, ideally, you want to hit two, three, sometimes even four inches behind the ball in the sand. Just how far behind depends on how far your shot has to go."

Another imporant distinction of a sand shot is that you

cannot ground your club (let the club touch the ground) to address the ball.

The rules of golf prohibit your setting the sole of your club down on the sand behind the ball as you set up for the shot. That's why you see players grip the club and take a few practice swings with it before they step into the trap. You hold your club slightly above the sand to address the ball in a bunker.

Another point of information about sand play you should know: if your ball lands in footprints some other player left, you have to play the ball from there. That's why you rake a trap after you finish hitting your shot. You can throw cigarettes, bottles and man-made objects out of a trap before you hit without a penalty, but not pebbles, leaves, sticks, or such. That's another point of the rules.

The rules of golf prohibit Hollis from setting the sole of her club down on the sand behind the ball to address the ball.

THE SWING

None of the pros has mastered getting out of a trap better than Sandra Palmer. Why not imitate her technique? "Take your grip, being a little more firm with the last three fingers of your left hand. That keeps firm control in your left hand to lead the shot. Open your stance, with your left foot back from your right, your body facing the target.

"Plant your feet down in the sand, rather than on it. That gives you a chance to feel the texture of the sand, to judge how hard you have to swing to get through it.

"Flex your knees. Feel your weight on your left foot. The ball should be just off your left heel. Cock your hands. Hold the club square to the ball just a little above the sand with your hands ahead of it.

"Using your shoulders, arms, and hands, take the club back and up immediately. There is little body movement in the swing. Think of it as a *V* or *U* shape."

How far do you hit behind the ball? How fast do you come through the shot? That depends on how far the ball has to go. Usually, if the pin is close, you take more sand and swing more slowly. If the pin is farther back, you take less sand and swing a little faster. In either case, be sure to follow through on the shot. Otherwise, the sand stops or slows down your swing.

The more you open up the face of the sand wedge, the more your ball will run and the lower it will run. Aim two inches behind the ball as an average. Open the clubface more if you want the ball to run on the green.

For shorter shots, with little run, close your clubface. The ball will bounce out and hold the green better.

Essentially, to swing a sand wedge, break your wrists and take the club away on the outside. Lift it up as sharply as you can with your arms and come down aiming to hit a spot in the sand behind the ball.

Most amateurs make too low a swing. That makes it harder to get the ball out of the sand.

To hit her ball out of sand from a steep hill, Sandra grips her club firmly with the last three fingers of her left hand. Then she opens her stance and plants her feet down in the sand with her weight on her left, the ball off her left foot. She cocks her hands just a little ahead of the ball and sets the club square with the ball just a little above the sand.

Keeping her body facing the target, Sandra brings the club back and up sharply with her shoulders, arms, and hands.

Notice that the top of Sandra's backswing is at the top of that V or U pattern she refers to for a bunker shot. How far she comes up depends on how far the ball has to go.

Coming down firmly, using little body movement, Sandra aims for a spot behind the ball.

Above, left: The flange on the bottom of Sandra's wedge enables her to hit the sand behind the ball to bounce the ball out of the bunker. With her weight on her left she has to swing smoothly and firmly. Above, right: Sandra completes her shot looking at the stick. If she had quit on the shot, her club would have stuck in the sand or not gone through firmly enough to get the ball out.

Remember, the swing for a sand shot is different from most others. It's a shoulders, arms, and hands swing. Break your wrists and bring the club back and up sharply, then down, smoothly and firmly.

YOUR AIM

"I hit about the same distance behind the ball for every shot—about 1½ inches," says Hollis. "I allow for the difference in distances by the angle I play my club. For long shots my club is more open. For my short shots I swing it with the face more upright."

"It is difficult to tell someone else how far to hit behind the ball," Sandra agrees. "If you want to play a little shot, either hit farther behind the ball or have less speed on the club as you come through the sand. For a longer shot, hit closer to the ball. Don't take as much sand."

SAND REVELATIONS

"When you practice, make sure that your divot in the sand is nice and smooth," points out Hollis. "It should look rectangular but not deep. Then you know you're using the flange of the wedge as you should. If the divot looks like you dug the club in at an angle, then you need to practice some more."

When Hollis takes a sand shot, her club leaves a smooth, rectangular divot in the sand. That indicates that she used her club correctly.

The consistency of sand changes with different locations in the same area and in different areas of the country. It can even differ from bunker to bunker on the same course. You have to expect that. It is difficult to analyze just how the ball is going to come out of some of them. Experience is your best teacher.

From some lies you're just not going to be able to hit a very good shot. The ball always tends to roll to the lowest point, which means that it often ends up in a hole. Don't let those shots get you down. Do the best you can. Sometimes the sand is of poor quality, full of pebbles and rocks. It's a poor bunker to play.

Remember, your first objective is to get out of the bunker. You don't always have to go forward to do so. If you can't manage to get the ball out the front way, go out sideways or even the back way.

When you walk into the bunker, think about how you are going to execute the shot. Why not approach it as Sandra does? "Walking in, I grip my left hand a little firmer. At address I'm conscious of my weight over on my left side. I cock my hands to lift the club a little sooner. I think, 'Aim for a spot and accelerate through the sand.' I key myself, repeating *firm* and *smooth*."

You can use those same key words to help your bunker play. Or perhaps you already have others in mind to use.

DIFFICULT SHOTS

When your ball is up against a steep bank, use an extremely open stance. Take less backswing and be certain the blade of your wedge hits squarely.

The lighter the sand, the farther behind the ball you can aim. Try a more open stance. With heavy sand, often wet, square your stance slightly. Hit right behind the ball. When the ball is below your feet, it is going to come out lower. You should stand closer to the ball than usual. Sandra suggests, "Play it back a little in your stance with your weight forward. Take an open stance with your left foot and body open to enable you to take the club back and up immediately. Concentrate on hitting that spot two inches behind the ball. Don't swing so hard that you lose your balance."

When your ball lands deep in the sand (a fried egg), close your clubface and play the ball back in your stance to get out. Keep your stance open, unless you have to hit the ball a long distance. If so, square your stance more. The farther the shot you have to make, the more you should stand square with the ball. You have to hit hard and firmly to get down in the sand.

If the ball is buried in the sand, consider using your pitching wedge to get it out. You can hit deeper into the sand. Hood the clubface (turn the top of the clubface forward) and swing hard to go down deep behind the ball.

If you find your ball right under the lip of a bunker, declare an unplayable lie. "It's dumb to stand there and take three or four shots trying to make an impossible one," comments Sandra. "You have the right to declare a lie unplayable. This is one place to do it. Take your penalty and give yourself a chance with your next shot."

When you declare an unplayable lie, you are allowed to drop the ball farther back in the bunker as long as you keep that point where the ball originally landed between you and the hole, taking a one-stroke penalty.

Would you use a wood out of a fairway bunker? Beth Daniel advises, "Never, unless you have a very good lie and the ball is on an upslope. It is one of the toughest shots in golf. If you catch the ball a little, then it's going to drive right down into the sand. You have to catch it perfectly, sweep it out perfectly. The majority of times, you're much better off using a four or five iron for such bunker play."

PRACTICE

The more you practice, the more you learn about bunker shots. You will find that you don't have to hit a perfect one every time for your ball to sneak out of the trap. If you hit a little behind where you meant to, the ball can pop out—

For a flat sand lie, Hollis has to be sure to bring her club back far enough to get the ball out and take enough sand not to sail it out. At the top of her backswing her weight is forward, her arms ready to lead her left hand down with her clubhead to a point in the sand behind the ball.

With her wrists about to un-cock, her weight forward, Hollis brings her clubface down slightly open, aiming for the spot behind the ball.

Breaking her wrists, Hollis accelerates her club through the sand behind the ball. She keeps extending to be certain that she doesn't quit on the shot.

Hollis finishes high to complete the shot and get the ball well onto the green.

though just barely. If you hit a little bit cleaner (take less sand) than you intended to, the ball will fly out—hopefully not over the green.

Keep practicing to make those perfect ones that land on the green, close to the cup, maybe even in it. Confidently hit a ball out of a bunker.

1. Use a club especially designed for bunker play.

2. Do not ground your club behind the ball when you address it.

3. Grip the club firmly with the last three fingers of your left hand to lead the swing.

4. Take an open stance with your body facing the target, your knees flexed, your weight on your left foot.

5. Position the ball off your left heel.

6. With your hands ahead of the ball, hold the club slightly above the sand to address the ball.

7. To swing, cock your wrists, using your shoulders, arms, and hands, and take the club back and up immediately.

8. *Most important:* Aim for a spot in the sand behind the ball.

9. Using the flange of the club, accelerate through the sand, bouncing the ball out.

10. Be sure to follow through.

12

Left-Handed Golfers

"Only think of yourself as a left-handed golfer when you're choosing equipment," advises Bonnie Bryant, the only left-handed player on the LPGA tour. "When you're playing golf, just play the hole the way you see it."

Because she plays golf left-handed, Bonnie is not able to try out manufacturers' new sample equipment as the other pros can. But that's the only limitation she's found in being a left-handed golfer.

EQUIPMENT

Actually, golf equipment for left-handed women today is far superior to the equipment available in those days early in her career when Bonnie "prayed a lot" to find any. "You have to look to find it, but it is there," she says encouragingly. "Right now it is probably as good as it's going to be until many, many more women are playing golf left-handed."

Bonnie's a popular instructor with right-handed players. Using terms like the hand toward the hole, *she gives them a mirror image to imitate.*

No doubt, the main advantage to playing golf right-handed is the availability of equipment. Right-handed golfers are able to try before they buy. Left-handed players have to special-order what they want, hoping they are going to like what they receive.

Certain manufacturers do make clubs for left-handed women golfers. Such companies include Cobra, Karsten-Ping, and Square Two. Square Two Golf Corporation, in New Jersey, carries the endorsement of the LPGA. All the companies have catalogs of what they make and are glad to furnish them upon request.

Golf shops do not stock left-handed equipment for the most part. Only the biggest outlets might have a few demonstrators that you could try to feel the swing.

If you can't find a shop with equipment you can try, look around and see what other left-handed women are playing with, Bonnie suggests. Ask them if you can swing their clubs to feel how the shaft reacts to your swing, how the swing weight feels to you. The more you know what you like in a club, the more information you can give when you do order your own clubs.

"This is where a club pro or a pro in a golf shop can help you," notes Bonnie. "He can suggest what he thinks you should order for your size and build and from what you tell him feels good to you in other clubs."

Right-handed gloves for left-handed players are also a problem to find sometimes. If you can't locate any, Bonnie wears Hogan, Palmer, and Titleist brands. Have your golf shop get in touch with them.

PLAY RIGHT- OR LEFT-HANDED?

Bonnie Bryant plays golf left-handed. Otherwise, she is right-handed. She started to play softball left-handed when she was in fourth grade. By the time she took up golf she was a left-handed athlete.

JoAnne Carner is naturally left-handed. She plays golf right-handed. So does left-handed Sally Little.

These women pros play the way they are most coordinated, most powerful. That's what you should do.

If you're just taking up golf and are left-handed, consider playing golf right-handed. You will start off at an advantage because you will be using your stronger side. But if you're not comfortable, play left-handed.

"Most instructors will try to switch a left-handed woman to play golf right-handed at first. Try it both ways," Bonnie recommends. "Then play whichever way you are the most coordinated, most comfortable. The average woman's game is based on coordination, rhythm, and tempo more than power."

But, if you are a left-handed teenager or young woman who is strong and well coordinated, Bonnie strongly encourages you to play golf right-handed. "You are going to be hitting with your strong side from the very beginning. That means you won't have the usual beginner's problems with slicing. You'll hit farther, easier, right from the start."

INSTRUCTION

You might think it better, if you're left-handed, to look for a left-handed instructor. "Not so," says Bonnie. "It is more convenient to go to a right-handed pro," she has found, "even though you have to reverse everything. If the pro says *right*, you think *left*. Perhaps you can get your instructor to use the phrases *front hand toward the hole* and *back hand toward the hole* in teaching you. Then you wouldn't have to reverse anything."

Bonnie tells left-handed golfers, "There is a decided advantage when a right-handed instructor faces a left-handed student during a lesson. You have a mirror image to follow, to imitate. You can follow so much more easily and the instructor doesn't have to run around to show you what to do."

Bonnie Bryant follows through on her swing just like any other pro. She never thinks of herself as a left-handed golfer until she needs a new piece of equipment.

When you read golf books, you do have to reverse the instruction. But if you watch the women pros on TV, Bonnie passes on a tip on how to do it that she got from left-handed golfer Gary Morton, Lucille Ball's husband, while they were playing a round together. "When you're watching a golf tournament on TV, watch it through a mirror. Then all the players golf left-handed, just like you."

ON THE COURSE

"When I step onto a tee, I automatically think, 'How am I going to have to play this hole?' " reveals Bonnie. "It has nothing to do with being left-handed or right-handed."

Most tees are more clear of bushes and tree branches and such on the right than on the left. That presents no problems for left-handed golfers as long as you are aware of it. Most golf courses are designed for right-handed players to have to work the ball left and then right. They have doglegs left and doglegs right.

"That works out basically the same for a left-handed player," Bonnie finds. "You just have to think the opposite of a right-handed player."

BE COMFORTABLE

"Don't ever let yourself feel uncomfortable because you are a left-handed player," Bonnie says emphatically. "You can handle your game as well as any right-handed player. A few situations can arise because you are left-handed, but you can handle them."

Develop your sense of humor. People do love to tease left-handed players.

If other players in your group seem unaware you are left-handed, it's better to make them conscious of it when you first start playing. You have a right to expect other players in your group to be out of your way, as you are out of theirs.

Until the caddies become accustomed to you, you might

have to ask them to back up a few times so you're not crowded on the tee.

"When you're playing a hole, play it as you see it," Bonnie reminds you. "The only difference between a good right-handed player and a good left-handed one is the look of their equipment."

13

The Rules and Courtesies of Golf

Many women have a lackadaisical attitude about playing golf according to the rules of the game. This is understandable. Learning to hit the ball comes first when you take up golf. Then you have to learn your way around a golf course. Before you can become interested in the rules of golf you have to start playing the game. But then you should learn the rules. It's your responsibility to learn the rules of any game you play.

There are times in any round when a question of rules can come up. During tournament play, knowing how to play the ball under unusual circumstances, according to the rules, can determine the outcome of the competition.

The United States Golf Association publishes a booklet, *The Rules of Golf.* It's readily available through pro shops and bookstores. Buy one the next time you have a chance.

It is difficult to pick up a rule book and just learn rules.

There are a lot of them and many are not easy to understand. But help is at hand. Marie Feeney, an expert on the rules of golf, explains some of the ones you might be confronted with in ordinary play. If you know these basic ones and understand them, you can handle many of the situations demanding knowledge of the rules that you will encounter.

To deal with problems that might come up in your regular play, she recommends that you know: the meaning of the phrase *nearest point that provides relief*; what an *unplayable lie* is and how you handle one; what happens when a ball goes *out of bounds*; what the difference between a *lateral water hazard* and a *water hazard* is when you hit your ball into water.

THE NEAREST POINT THAT PROVIDES RELIEF

What does a *free lift* mean, when do you get one, and what does it have to do with the *nearest point that provides relief*?

You don't have to play your ball from: casual water (a temporary accumulation of water that is visible before or after a player takes her stance and is not in a water hazard); ground that's under repair (as designated by the committee or its authorized representative); a hole made by a burrowing animal; or an obstruction, such as a cart path.

Without a penalty, you can lift the ball from that spot and drop it within one club length of the point that provides relief and: a) is not nearer the hole; b) avoids interference by the condition; c) is not in a hazard or on a putting green. That's a *free lift*. You can check the rule being applied for other specific conditions governing your situation.

A free lift allows you one club length, no nearer the hole from the point thus determined, to find a better place to play your shot without a penalty. A penalty adds a stroke to your score.

The rule doesn't state that the one club length from the nearest point that provides relief must offer you a good swing or a stance or good ball placement. Sometimes it doesn't.

The handles of the golf clubs point to the ball that landed on a cart path. When your ball lands on a cart path, you have a free lift. You can drop the ball within one club length of the point that provides relief no nearer the hole, without taking a penalty. In this case that nearest point that provides relief would be to the left. To the right would not be the nearest point.

That's when confusion arises.

You cannot assume that, if the one club length from the nearest point of relief doesn't offer relief from some other problem, you can get it elsewhere. Not so. You can't play the ball from the point that gives you the best shot. You must play it within one club length of the nearest point that provides relief from the situation governed by the rule you are applying.

UNPLAYABLE LIE

What is an *unplayable lie*? How do you handle one? Is there a penalty?

When your ball lands in a place where there is no possible way you can play it, you can declare the ball unplayable. That allows you, taking a one-stroke penalty, to choose a way that you can play the ball. You have three options.

1. You can drop the ball within two club lengths of the point where the ball lies, no nearer the hole, to play your shot. Lift your ball from the unplayable lie, such as against a tree. Holding the ball in your hand, with your arm extended straight out at shoulder height, drop the ball *within* the two club lengths' relief, no closer to the hole. Face any direction, stand as necessary, to be certain the ball is dropped within that two club lengths' relief area, no closer to the hole.

When your ball wedges up against a tree, you can declare an unplayable lie. Then, taking a one-stroke penalty, drop the ball within two club lengths of where the ball landed, no closer to the hole, for your next shot.

2. You can choose to go back as far as you want from where the ball lies, when the two-club-length option doesn't give the relief you need to make a shot. You must keep the point where the ball came to rest between yourself and the hole. But you can go as far back on that line as you wish, unless you are in a bunker.

In Chapter 11, on bunker play, referring to a ball landing under the lip of a trap, it stated that a player can declare an unplayable lie in such a circumstance. You take the penalty and drop the ball back farther in the bunker to make your next shot, still keeping the point where the ball lay between you and the hole.

Hitting a ball from a hazard involves another rule of the game. When a ball lies in a bunker—or within an area

When your ball lands in the middle of a clump of bushes instead of on the green and there is no relief available within two club lengths, you declare the ball unplayable. Taking a one-stroke penalty, you can drop the ball as far back as you like from where the ball landed, as long as you keep that spot between yourself and the hole when you make your next shot.

distinctively marked by stakes as part of a lateral water hazard or water hazard—you cannot touch the ground in the hazard to set up for your shot. You cannot ground your club in back of the ball to address it.

Another example of the option for an unplayable lie, allowing you to go as far back as you want from where the ball lies, would be if your ball landed in the middle of a clump of bushes. You can hit your next shot behind the point where the ball came to rest, keeping that spot between yourself and the hole, with no limit to how far behind that point you may drop the ball.

3. You can choose to go back to where you originally hit the shot to make your next one. That option is necessary when the two club lengths offer no relief and it is impossible to keep the point where the ball lies between yourself and the hole to make a shot. That could happen if you hit your ball into a section of bushes in front of a number of trees in the rough off a fairway of a hole.

OUT OF BOUNDS

When golf started, players just hit the ball and kept hitting it until they put it into a cup. But now courses are built in cities on limited acreage. Rules are necessary to guide players on how to handle today's golf course limitations.

"When a ball goes *out of bounds* (generally marked by white stakes or fences) most golfers go to see if it's really out," Marie observes. "When it is, instead of going back to the tee or to wherever the shot was hit to play the next one, the woman drops a ball where she is. That's not what the rule says. The penalty for going out of bounds is losing the distance as well as the stroke."

If you're not certain your ball went out of bounds, declare you are hitting a provisional ball. Then do it before leaving the tee. If you find your first ball, pick up the provisional. (Check the rule book for limitations governing play of a provisional ball.)

When your ball lands beyond a white stake, it's out-of-bounds. That means you lose distance and stroke. You have to go back to where you hit your shot to play your next one. In this example, you would have to go back to the tee. You would be hitting your third shot.

LATERAL WATER HAZARD

"With a *lateral water hazard*, generally defined by red stakes and/or lines, when a ball splashes into the water, Mrs. Average Golfer frequently takes out another ball and drops it opposite the point where the ball splashed into the water to play her next shot. But she shouldn't," says Marie.

"The rule states that for a lateral water hazard the ball should be dropped within two club lengths opposite the point where the ball last crossed the margin of the hazard. That margin could be 50 yards back from where the ball splashed into the water. The margin should be defined by stakes or lines or both. It extends vertically upward. So where the ball crosses that boundary line is where it enters the hazard, not where the ball splashes into the water."

For a lateral water hazard, which usually runs parallel to the fairway, you can drop your ball within two club lengths of the stakes or lines where the ball crossed. Or you can choose to drop it on the other side of the water hazard at a point equidistant from the hole. In most cases this means that you don't have to hit over the water to make your next shot.

If you prefer, you can choose to play your ball using the same options offered under the water hazard rule.

When your ball crosses the margin of a lateral water hazard, you drop your ball within two club lengths of the stakes or lines where the ball crossed the margin.

WATER HAZARD

A *water hazard* is usually marked by yellow stakes and/or lines. It frequently runs across a fairway or is directly in front of a green.

When the water is defined as a water hazard, you do have to hit over the water again if your ball goes in. That is, if your ball goes into the water when you hit it initially, you have to keep the point where the ball last crossed the margin of the hazard between you and the hole to hit your next shot. You are not allowed to go to either side of the water. But you can play the ball from the spot where you played the original ball.

LEARNING RULES

When you're out playing a relaxing nine with your husband or boyfriend or enjoying a round with your friends, this is the time to learn the rules. Discuss unusual situations and check your rules book for the answers. If you need help, talk the problem over with the club's rules committee or pick up a copy of Tom Watson's book on rules.

It's up to you to learn the rules of golf so you can play the game as it's intended to be played. No doubt, you've heard of times when knowing the rules won or lost a game. Give yourself every opportunity. The rules provide advantages as well as penalties. Don't ever let not knowing a rule stand between you and the excitement of winning.

COURTESY ON THE COURSE

Extend courtesy on the golf course just as you would anywhere else. It's part of the spirit of the game.

If you lose a ball in some bushes, look for it. But, if after a few minutes, you don't find it, invite the players following you to play through while you continue to look. You have five minutes to find the ball. Then it is a lost ball, whether you subsequently find it or not.

When play is slow, don't provoke the group in front to step livelier by hitting your balls right up behind them. If you sincerely believe they are playing too slowly, ask to go through them. If the hole is open in front of them, they should allow you to do that. But, if there is nowhere you can go, they need not agree to your request.

SLOW PLAY

Slow play can ruin the fun of a game and absolutely destroy concentration. If your group is slow, you know it. See if you can't get them to move along. It's not hard.

Be up to the ball when it's your turn to hit. Whether you're walking or in a cart, get up to your ball *before* it's your turn. No, you don't stand in front of players who are hitting. But you can stand off to the side of the fairway ahead of them in line with your ball. When the player behind you finishes her shot you are ready to go to your ball.

The important point is to keep your eye on the player who is hitting—anywhere. It is not necessary to stay far behind in order to do that.

More and more women are playing golf now. It's important to everyone's enjoyment to keep play moving.

Score your hole on the next tee, not when you walk off the green.

There may be women in your group who get lost in chatter about last night's party or the kids' troubles at school as they walk down the fairway or wait on the tee. Sometimes it seems that they are more interested in talking than in playing. It becomes a problem when they slow down their pace to talk. That forces the whole field behind you to slow down. It's tricky to handle. You don't want to offend your friends. Try to mention how your group is slowing down. More directly, interrupt the conversation to say, "I must get up to my ball but would love to hear all about it at lunch." Hopefully, the conversationalist will take the hint.

Heavy conversation belongs on the 19th hole. To play well,

give your game your full attention. By now, you know that making good golf shots demands concentration.

CART COOPERATION

Cart driving on the golf course is an art. It takes cart cooperation to play along smoothly and at a good pace. When you take your partner to her ball, drive on to yours or in line with it. She can walk up to the cart after she hits, while you ready your shot.

For the next shot your ball might be the closer of the two. Get out of the cart with the clubs you might need, taking two or three if you have a question, so you don't have to go back and forth to the cart for others. Your partner can drive on to her ball. After you've hit your shot you can walk to the cart and get a little exercise.

COURSE MAINTENANCE

Golf course maintenance is an endless chore. But thoughtful players can help a lot.

Drive your cart in the rough whenever possible. Don't bring it right up alongside the greens or tee areas, rolling over the hills around them.

Replace your divots and those you see that other players neglected on the fairways. Rake the traps when you're finished. Smooth over your footprints, holes, and such. You can throw out man-made debris, like cigarette butts or cans, that doesn't belong there.

Repair the ball mark that your ball made on the green when it landed, as well as others that might be there. Walk with an agile step so your shoes won't leave spike marks that can interfere with the next group's putts. As you're leaving the green, repair the spike marks that you see.

Don't neglect to replace the flagstick in the cup correctly when your finish a hole. Leaving it at an angle, rubbing against the edge of the cup, damages the hole, and takes away its sharp edge.

If perchance, your shot goes wild, shout "Fore." That tells the people toward whom the ball is heading to duck, or at least to look out. Of course, that is just an afterthought. When you imitate the pro golfers you don't hit wild shots.

14
Equipment

You want to buy a set of golf clubs now that you're seriously taking up the game. Or you're not happy with the ones you have. You plan to look for a new set.

Your timing is perfect. Now, as never before, there is a wide choice of clubs—*especially designed for women golfers*—on the market. Only in the last five years have manufacturers actually started making clubs designed for women players. Until then, clubheads designed for men's clubs were adapted for women. The same mold for a man's clubhead was used for a woman's. Sometimes a different button was screwed on the back of it to change its look a little. Then, with a shorter shaft and a woman's emblem stuck on the clubhead, presto—it became a club for a woman.

Lynx Golf Equipment in California was the first manufacturer to acknowledge that there is no way a woman has the power to swing a club like a man, that there was a need for lighter clubs women could swing easily. They introduced the first clubs actually designed for a woman's golf game. They sold hundreds of thousands and continue to upgrade that original design. Now a number of other equipment manufacturers also make excellent clubs for women.

Your problem will be to select the best for you. That's an interesting problem.

CLUBS

If you know nothing about golf clubs, there are a few facts that will help you understand the lingo used in golf shops about equipment.

When you say you want to buy a set of golf clubs, that implies that you want to buy the woods and the irons. You can also buy a set of woods or a set of irons separately. Or you can buy individual clubs in some shops.

The number on the club indicates its degree of loft—the backward slant of the face of the clubhead. The higher the number on the club, the greater its loft. When you look, you can see that a nine iron has a more lofted clubface than a four iron. A seven wood has a more lofted clubhead than a three wood.

The basic difference between clubs is the distance they hit a ball as well as the trajectory (how high in the air) they put on a ball.

There is about a 10-yard difference between two consecutive clubs. For instance, if you can hit a five iron 100 yards, you'll probably hit a six iron 90 yards, a four iron 110 yards. Your friend won't necessarily hit a five iron the same distance you do. But she will have that same 10-yard difference in how far she does hit each club, if she has developed her swing.

This gradation means you don't have to ease up on a club or hit it any harder to arrive at the distance you want. Your swing remains the same with little modification. You choose the club you want to use based on how far you want to hit the ball.

WHERE TO BUY

Golf clubs are sold either in pro shops or in stores. A pro shop is a golf store usually at a golf facility—municipal course, driving range, private club, or such.

Basically, the prices are the same and the clubs are the same. But you won't find the clubs under the same name. For instance, though they are very similar, Wilson stocks Patty Berg Pro clubs in pro shops and Laura Baugh Classic clubs in stores.

In the pro shops you do not have to buy the whole set of clubs at one time. They carry open stock. In the stores, there is no open stock. You cannot buy part of the set at one time and go get the rest later.

Often you can get a better price on clubs from a store. But you will probably get better service, more personal attention, at a pro shop.

WOMEN'S CLUBS

When you go to look for your set of golf clubs you'll find that the manufacturer's basic set for women is generally made up of four woods and six irons plus a wedge. If the set has four woods, in the current market they will include the driver, three, five, and seven woods. In the past, and still available, the set included the driver, three, four, and five woods. There are also three-wood sets with a driver, three, and five woods only.

The basic iron set now marketed runs through the four, five, six, seven, eight, and nine irons plus a utility wedge. But there are sets made up of a three, four, five six, seven, eight, and nine iron plus a pitching wedge and a sand wedge.

This gives you an idea of the wide selection on hand. That's why it's good to know something about clubs before you go in to buy.

If you were to ask Nancy Lopez to recommend a set of golf clubs for an average woman's play, she would suggest a set made up with five woods and five irons plus three wedges. Her wood choices include the driver, three, five, and seven wood, plus a trouble wood; her irons, the five, six, seven, eight, and nine, plus a pitching wedge, sand wedge, and utility wedge. She feels these would be easy clubs for any woman to use, especially if she is looking for a good time playing golf with her friends and is not too strong or interested in developing the skills of the game.

You buy your putter in addition to these clubs. It is not part of a set. But you can't get the ball in the hole without one.

STARTER SETS

If you're just starting to play, think about buying a starter set to learn the game—a five, seven, and nine iron, plus a five wood and a putter. You don't need a full set of clubs to learn to swing a golf club. You won't use them.

While you are learning to hit your seven iron, it will fly a ball anywhere from 25 to 75 yards. When you get to the point where you get a consistent distance—about 80 yards, for example, using your seven iron—then you'll want a six and an eight iron in your set. You'll want them because you will have developed a good enough swing to give you different distances using different clubs. That can take one season or many. It depends on you and the time you can spend.

You can use that five wood off the tee and for all your fairway shots, as long as you want to.

Marlene Floyd said she really got her swing going with a five wood. "Most women can hit a five wood off the tee a nice distance. It's a fun and easy club to hit."

Some women buy inexpensive starter sets. Others buy registered clubs. That means you can buy clubs to match in the same pattern when you are ready to buy the clubs to complete your set.

You don't have to invest much money initially when you buy a starter set. After you've played for a while you have a better idea of what you want when you do buy your complete set.

HOW TO SHOP

The most important thing to do when you shop for golf clubs is to swing the clubs you are considering. Swing the demonstrator or the clubs in the set you like. Feel the difference between them and the clubs in other sets.

As excellent as she is off the tee, Beth Daniel notes that there are certain woods she can't hit. If that is true for the LPGA's first $200,000 season winner, it certainly is true for any amateur.

You'll find you swing some woods easily. Others won't feel right at all. Design and quality make the difference.

Manufacturers have a specific type of woman golfer in mind when they design their women's clubs. What is put out for a beginner differs markedly from the club marketed for a woman who shoots in the high 80s (handicap of 15 or below).

When you go to a shop to pick out a set of clubs, the pro can see how tall you are, what your general build is. There are club measurement sticks available in pro shops that tell you how long your clubs should be, based on the length of your arms and your height.

After you describe what kind of a golfer you are, the pro should be able to help you make a wise choice of clubs, especially suited to you. That's why it's passé for your boyfriend or husband to pick out a "nice" set of clubs for you. Let him buy them—but you should pick them out.

If you don't know any pros, call pro shops and stores in your area until you find one who is willing to spend time with you to help you make your selection.

SWING WEIGHT

None of the pros on the LPGA tour swing heavy clubs. But thousands of amateur women golfers do.

"Most women swing clubs much too heavy for them," points out Sally Little. "Their swings are loose at the top because their little wrists can't hold the club up there. The clubhead is too heavy."

The first thing you notice when you pick up a club is how heavy it feels. "Don't get a heavy golf club," Judy Rankin advises. "The most important consideration is overall weight. My driver weighs less than 12 ounces, which is very light. I would think all women at the amateur level would want a club that is light."

Actually, swing weight is the factor on which to base your weight selection. Swing weight measures what you feel when you swing a club. A set of clubs with good swing weight all feel and swing the same, regardless of how you grip the club, as long as you grip each club the same way.

Swing weight is indicated by letters and numbers in the manufacturers' brochures. The lighest clubs are lettered C, with numbers from 0 through 9; medium are D, 0 through 9; E are the heaviest. A good swing weight for a woman generally is from C, 7 through 9, or perhaps D, 0.

Total weight is what you feel when you pick up the club. In a very good set of clubs each iron will weigh the same as every other iron in the set. Each wood will weigh the same as every other wood in the set.

LENGTH, BALANCE, PERCUSSION

"A woman also needs the correct length of club with the correct balance," Sally Little adds. "How many times have you heard a woman say, 'I love my seven iron, but I can't hit my six iron'? You know why that is? The club is not balanced correctly for her. I think that is going to be the new breakthrough in clubs for women—clubs that are well balanced, with longer shafts and lighter clubheads."

With the new clubs coming on the market, two-thirds of the women buying clubs will be able to use the lengths available. But, if not, you can special-order what you need, for a slight extra charge.

Actually, the kind of clubs Sally talks about as a "breakthrough" have arrived. Square Two Equipment in New Jersey is manufacturing totally matched clubs for women. Totally

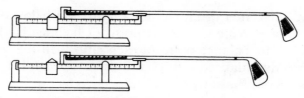

1. Matched Swingweight

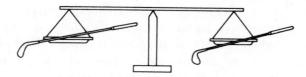

2. Matched Total Weight

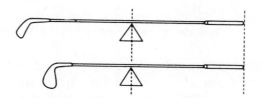

3. Matched Centers of Gravity

4. Matched Centers of Percussion

Golf clubs should be precision instruments, finely engineered, and rigidly quality controlled to produce clubs with optimum performance.

matched means matched swing weight, matched total weight, matched center of gravity (balance), and matched center of percussion (point to hit ball best).

To find the center of gravity on a club, you balance the shaft on your finger. Note where the point of balance is. Then line up the set. The balance point of each club is in the same place on a perfectly balanced set. That means you can hit each club in that set as well as any other club.

Another technical point that might interest you is the center of percussion on a club. That is the point on the head of the club where it is best to hit the ball. A set of clubs that maintains this center of percussion exactly where it belongs on each clubhead gives you additional yardage with less effort than the set whose center of percussion ranges from the tip of the clubhead on one club to up on the shaft on another. You can't count on such clubs for good, easy distance.

CHOICE OF WOODS

The beauty of woods goes beyond inlaid wood and color patterns.

If you're an experienced golfer, carrying a low handicap (15 or below), you want a clubhead with rigid tolerances built in that will give you solid feel in your hands when you swing the club. The toe of the clubhead might look like a man's. But there's distinct difference in weight, length, and grip specifications in the club.

If you're just getting your game going, you don't need to spend the money for quality in your woods that more experienced players seek. But do look for a wide metal insert on your woods. You need that bigger hitting area.

If you shoot between 90 and 115, look for a wood that has features to improve your game. You want a light clubhead that is compact and maneuverable. *Investment-cast* means it has more adherence to rigid tolerances and gives you a solid feel. A wood that is *perimeter weighted* offers you a larger sweet spot and boasts a low center of gravity.

Ram has a line of *keel-soled* woods now. The bottom of the sole of the woods comes down to a point similar to those on trouble woods. The company believes that this new feature

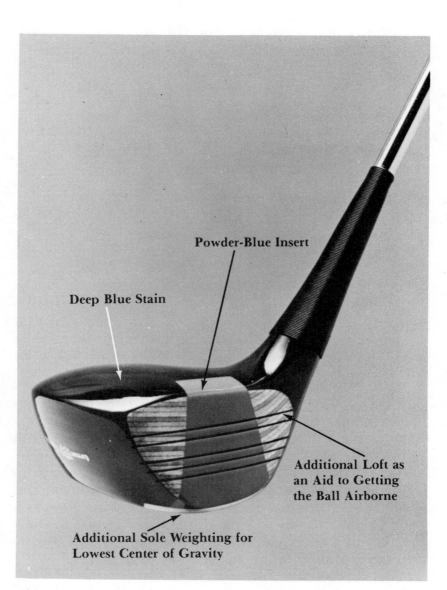

Powder-Blue Insert

Deep Blue Stain

Additional Loft as an Aid to Getting the Ball Airborne

Additional Sole Weighting for Lowest Center of Gravity

This picture shows how a special investment-cast metal alloy combined with the finest hardwood makes a solid, durable club. Because they are investment-cast, there are no inserts to crack or fall out and no neck whipping to unravel. The powder-blue color on the loft of the face marks the large sweet spot that gives the club perimeter weighting and a low center of gravity, all of which give you more control for even your most difficult shots.

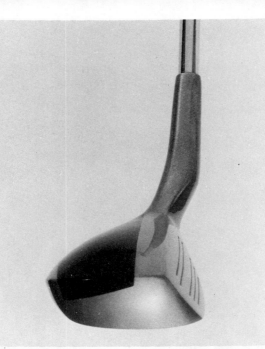

In this close-up of a wood, notice how the manufacturer has built "offset" into the club. The position of the hosel (socket) for the shaft on the clubhead is designed so that your hands are in front of the ball. This positioning helps you achieve solid ball contact.

will make it easier for women to consistently hit straight, far shots with their woods.

Wilson's new Tiara line stresses a contour grip and offset in all its clubs.

The grip of the club is an important factor to look at in both woods and irons. If the grip is too big, you won't be able to get any feel in your hands from it. The Tiara features a grip designed to the contour of a woman's hand. Other manufacturers stress not only size, but the material used to help you manipulate your club better as well.

Manufacturers put offset in a club because they believe that makes it easier for you to keep your hands ahead of the ball and to hit the ball solidly. If the set has offset in its woods, it is also in its irons.

IRONS

Sometimes the irons in the set for a low-handicap woman

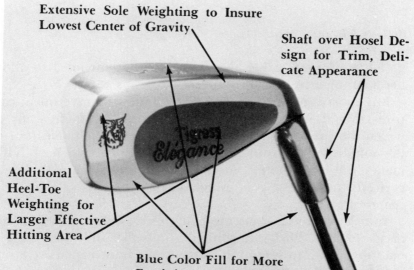

Extensive Sole Weighting to Insure Lowest Center of Gravity

Shaft over Hosel Design for Trim, Delicate Appearance

Additional Heel-Toe Weighting for Larger Effective Hitting Area

Blue Color Fill for More Feminine Appearance

Shaft and Grip Designed for Ladies Only

This close-up of an iron reveals the wider sole (bottom) of the newer women's clubs. Club weight is not increased, though. In fact, it's lighter. The weight has also been redistributed by the design of the club cavity—indicated by the darker color on the back of the clubhead. The size of this cavity reflects the wide sweet spot on the face of the club. As you can see, the club is also offset designed. Using this type of iron means you get the ball up in the air quicker and easier.

golfer are forged rather than cast. That is intended to allow her a stronger feel for the club in her hands.

But most amateurs do better playing with investment-cast irons. Metal is poured into the clubhead of these irons to widen the sweet spot. That means the weight is moved out of the middle of the iron and put into the toe and heel. That makes the club more forgiving. You don't have to hit it as perfectly to have a good shot. These irons also keep a low center of gravity.

You can tell the irons are cast this way if you look at the back of them. There are configurations that indicate a weight rearrangement in the club. These are more expensive irons than those for beginners.

For the aspiring player, the irons have a flange rim on the back to keep the center of gravity low. The clubs are sole-weighted to get the ball airborne easier. The toe of the iron is thicker than the heel. The sweet spot is wider. All these factors work together to make the irons easier to hit.

SHAFTS

The shaft is the most important part of a woman's club. Given equal clubhead weight, the more flexible the shaft, the more it will help you get clubhead speed. The stiffer the shaft, the more it will help accuracy.

Women need more flexibility in the shafts of their clubs than men do. *Flex* is the term used to describe the bend in the shaft. When you swing the club you feel flex more than you see it. The club will feel whippy or stiff. You swing the club to feel the differences and to find the shaft that is best for you.

You want a good lightweight one that will put spin on your ball, keep it straight, help it stay in the air longer and travel truer. That is why the shaft is so important.

CLUBS FOR SPECIAL GOLFERS

Cobra, Karsten-Ping, and Square Two now make clubs for left-handed women golfers.

Square Two, the manufacturer endorsed by the LPGA, also offers a set of clubs designed for the petite woman golfer, five feet three inches or shorter. They are lighter and shorter than conventional ladies' clubs. They are six to seven swing weight points lighter and 1½ inches shorter in total length. The shafts are specially cut for greater flexibility. These are a tremendous boost for the small woman's game.

THE RIGHT CLUBS

Keep looking until you find the set of clubs that feel just great to you. When you swing them you feel they were made for you.

On that line of thought, Judy Rankin has a suggestion for the low-handicap player who seriously intends to work on her game. "Once you have developed your golf swing and want to develop your skills even more, if you're going to invest in a set of good golf clubs, it doesn't cost that much more to have them custom-made." There's an idea you might want to look into.

However, it's possible for you to buy clubs in a set that have perfect total weight, swing weight, center of gravity, and percussion. Because they are so precisely engineered, they do cost more than other clubs.

Your choice should depend on what you can afford, on what kind of a game you play, and on what you seek from your clubs. There are clubs made to satisfy any woman's needs.

Be aware. Clubs are on the market whose only qualification for being women's clubs is a little emblem on the clubhead. They aren't good enough for you.

You want clubs especially designed for a woman golfer of your ability. Look for lightweight clubs with flexible shafts that swing easily and well for you.

CARE OF EQUIPMENT

Good golf clubs deserve good care. Don't expose your clubs to extreme temperatures. Cold hardens the grips. Heat and moisture damage the woods. That's why it's not a good idea to store them in the trunk of your car through the season.

If you do get caught in the rain on the course, be sure to dry off your woods when you get in. And check to see that the insides of the head covers aren't damp, before you put them back on the woods. You do need covers to keep the woods from being nicked or scarred.

Try to keep your clubs clean when you're playing. Those towels you can attach to your bag are handy. Dirty irons can't put a spin on the ball. Warm, soapy water is your best overall cleaner, plus a leather conditioner for your grips.

When you store your clubs, rub a lightweight oil on the clubheads of your irons to prevent rust. If you can, put your clubs flat on the floor to store them.

When your grips become shoddy with wear or your woods get tacky, you can have the grips relaced and the woods refinished or rewhipped.

Take care of your clubs. You can't play golf without them. They become familiar old friends when you have played with them for a long time.

EQUIPMENT MANUFACTURERS

Cobra Golf
11045 Sorrento Valley Ct.
San Diego, CA 92121

Ram Golf
2020 Indian Boundary Dr.
Melrose Park, IL 60160

Karsten-Ping
2201 W. Desert Cove
Phoenix, AZ 85029

Square Two Golf
140 Clinton Rd.
Fairfield, NJ 07006

Lynx Precision Golf
7302 Adams St.
Paramount, CA 90723

Wilson Golf
2233 West St.
River Grove, IL 60171

Index